ALSO BY JOHN ANDREW CARROLL
(writing as John Carroll)

Purposeful

Leading for an Engaged Culture

How the Lion Learned to Lead
and Other Stories

The 30 Natural Laws of Leadership
Explored Through African Animal Fables

John Andrew Carroll

BALBOA.PRESS
A DIVISION OF HAY HOUSE

Copyright © 2023 John Andrew Carroll.

All rights reserved. No part of this book may be used or reproduced by any means, graphic, electronic, or mechanical, including photocopying, recording, taping or by any information storage retrieval system without the written permission of the author except in the case of brief quotations embodied in critical articles and reviews.

Balboa Press books may be ordered through booksellers or by contacting:

Balboa Press
A Division of Hay House
1663 Liberty Drive
Bloomington, IN 47403
www.balboapress.com.au
AU TFN: 1 800 844 925 (Toll Free inside Australia)
AU Local: (02) 8310 7086 (+61 2 8310 7086 from outside Australia)

Because of the dynamic nature of the Internet, any web addresses or links contained in this book may have changed since publication and may no longer be valid. The views expressed in this work are solely those of the author and do not necessarily reflect the views of the publisher, and the publisher hereby disclaims any responsibility for them.

The author of this book does not dispense medical advice or prescribe the use of any technique as a form of treatment for physical, emotional, or medical problems without the advice of a physician, either directly or indirectly. The intent of the author is only to offer information of a general nature to help you in your quest for emotional and spiritual well-being. In the event you use any of the information in this book for yourself, which is your constitutional right, the author and the publisher assume no responsibility for your actions.

Any people depicted in stock imagery provided by Getty Images are models, and such images are being used for illustrative purposes only. Certain stock imagery © Getty Images.

Print information available on the last page.

ISBN: 978-1-9822-9737-4 (sc)
ISBN: 978-1-9822-9738-1 (e)

Balboa Press rev. date: 05/23/2023

For my late mum, Jean Ann Carroll,
who taught me early in life that leaders
are those who are willing to serve.

CONTENTS

Setting the Scene.. ix
Introduction..xvii

How the Lion Learned to Lead 1
How the Rhinoceros Got its Skin 23
How the Meerkats Formed a Family 37
How the Elephant Got its Trunk 53
How the Leopard Got its Spots 67
How the Monkey was Heard.. 83

Conclusion 95
About John Andrew Carroll 99
Acknowledgements...101

SETTING THE SCENE

AN AFRICAN UPBRINGING

This is a book of fables, fictional stories about African animals. You can read them just for their entertainment value, and for the messages they carry about a set of fundamental leadership principles that will help you in your work and life in general. But before we get into that, I want to give you some background so you understand what's behind these stories.

Growing up surrounded by wildlife in Zimbabwe in southern Africa was a magical experience for a young boy. Our home in the smallish town of Mutare, then "Umtali", in the eastern highlands of the country, was an ever-flowing menagerie of dogs, tame and wild birds, tortoises, butterflies, chameleons, baby antelope, monkeys, bush babies, snakes, and any other wildlife from around the area that we found, or that ended up with us after being orphaned, or injured, or having fallen out the nest.

My brothers, Tony, Simon, and I would spend countless

hours exploring the forests, mountains and foothills that sloped down behind our home suburb. To our frustration, my mum and dad wouldn't let us have a baby lion, or leopard, or the chimpanzee that I so desperately wanted in my young naivety. I thought it was very heartless of them!

But with the other wildlife in our garden and around the area, that wasn't a total tragedy. The bird life was incredible; vervet monkeys watched us, chattering from the trees; dassies scurried around on the ledges and crevices of the craggy rock faces of the nearby hills; butterflies flitted everywhere in profusion; other insects and small creatures abounded, just asking to be watched and wondered about; we'd frequently startle a duiker or some other antelope from its browsing in the scrub or woodlands.

Walking our dogs in the bushland and mountain foothills around my home town was always an adventure. In our early days in Mutare, there were leopards in the hills that edged the town's northern suburbs, and a dog was occasionally taken from a backyard. Our own dogs sometimes cornered a cobra or some other snake innocently going about its business, forcing it to defend itself. Our role in those dramas was to protect the dogs *and* the snake.

A large troop of baboons lived in the rocky outcrops above Christmas Pass, the winding section of road that crested the mountain behind our house, and then ran on two and a half hours northwest to Harare. The baboons sometimes stalked us at a distance, looking for an opportunity to pick off a wayward dog. And, of course, the dogs were always looking for an opportunity to pick off a wayward baboon! Fortunately, neither species was ever lucky enough to succeed, though, without doubt, the dogs would have lost

SETTING THE SCENE

any battle—Chacma Baboons are the largest member of the monkey family, and are strong, smart, fearless hunters.

It was an exciting, fascinating place to grow up, but in the background to it all was the grim reality of the Rhodesian civil war—the forces of the Shona tribe under Robert Mugabe, against the forces of the Matabele tribe under Joshua Nkomo, and both of those against the forces of the minority white government under Ian Smith.

That war raged from the time I was five until I was 20. Mutare is right on the border of Mozambique, where Robert Mugabe had his main military bases. Our school was 600 metres from the border.

Sitting in class, we'd often hear land mines exploding in the minefield that protected the town from direct invasion. A few times, Mugabe's forces fired across our sports fields while we were training, and our teachers had to rush us to cover in the rugby pavilion, which I believe shows the scars of those episodes to this day.

I learned to fire a rifle and a pistol at the age of 12 and would sometimes literally ride shotgun if I went out of town any distance with one of my parents. A number of my farming schoolmates lost parents, or were themselves injured when they hit a landmine, or when their farmhouse was attacked, or when they were ambushed driving to, from, or on their farm. Fortunately, none of my immediate friends were killed in this way while they were still at school, and we were never attacked when I was staying with farming friends on weekends or during the school holidays.

It may sound strange, but the war seemed just a normal part of life. I grew up with it and it was all I knew. And the story I have in my head is always of an idyllic childhood…

Idyllic until that childhood was shattered when Tony, my older brother, was killed in action in the army and I was conscripted less than six months later into national service, as was every white male when they reached the age of 18 and left school. Nine months after Tony's death, I was a sergeant in the same unit and in the same area in which Tony had lost his life at the age of 19.

In some ways, national service forced me to grow up fast and, of course, Tony's death had an enormous impact on me and my family. You never really get over that sort of thing.

Though I found the violence of war abhorrent and hated my time in the army, I know I learned something about people and leadership from those early experiences. It fed my already deep interest in people and the human condition, and that has helped me throughout my life, especially when founding and running my own advertising agency, and later, in Australia, in business and community leadership roles, and as a CEO.

And the images and stories of an idyllic childhood remain in my head to this day.

THE POWER OF STORIES

It's interesting how our stories define us. Neuro-science research is now showing us we all quite literally create our own concept of the world—our own unique sense of reality—based on the stories and associations we ingrain in our minds, often sub-consciously, from the time we're born and as we go on through life. So we live our entire lives subconsciously conjuring up, in any given situation, stories, images, and associations that fit with our past experiences, and then we react or respond accordingly.

That's the power of stories and imagination. They hugely influence our everyday beliefs, actions, and reactions. So, two people can witness the same events at the same time in a particular situation, and will often see, feel, and interpret those events completely differently. How each of them perceives the situation depends on the unique set of stories each individual has ingrained in their mind, and each one then creates their own story around that set of events. Those differing perspectives are the root cause of so much conflict between people, communities, and countries.

And, of course, we now know how powerful stories are in learning, in creating and sustaining a culture, in defining how we see and interact with other people.

All of which creates an intriguing and complex backdrop for leadership—and we're all leaders in some sense and in some situations, in our work, in our families, in clubs, in our friendship groups. How do you lead a group of people when each of them has a uniquely different view of the world and their place in it, a different perspective on their work, their life, and the people around them?

The combination of all that I've just related—my upbringing in Africa, my love of wildlife, my experience as a leader both in the army and in business, and my fascination with psychology and the human condition—is what drove and inspired me to write this book.

I love storytelling, and I hope the stories in this book entertain and inspire you.

INTRODUCTION

A DIFFERENT PHILOSOPHY

The fables in this book outline a philosophy of leadership that is much needed in today's world. Many organisations and their management teams are battling to adjust from the traditional view of leadership that pervaded the industrial era and much of the 20th century. But that approach to leadership simply doesn't work anymore... if it ever did.

That authoritarian form of leadership came from two underlying beliefs:

1. That the success of an organisation comes principally from having efficient and effective processes; and
2. That unless people are strictly monitored and controlled, they will not work productively.

These two flawed beliefs became a self-fulfilling prophecy, and the results were used to further justify authoritarian and dictatorial management styles. When people in an organisation of any sort don't want to be there and, instead of *wanting* to fulfil their role, feel forced to perform what to them are boring, repetitive, or unfulfilling functions, many will either rebel and leave, or reluctantly follow orders because they need the job and the money. Then, naturally, productivity falls since staff turnover is high, and those who stay tend to do only enough to avoid being fired. For management, that requires greater control over each employee's performance of their function… and the cycle goes on.

There is considerable research that confirms this. Gallup, in their "State of the Global Workplace: 2022 Report", a survey across over 160 countries, found that only 21% of employees globally are engaged in their work— Gallup defines employee engagement as "the involvement and enthusiasm of employees in their work and workplace".

It's important to note that these findings are not simply a reflection of the COVID-19 pandemic. For example, the 2017 Gallup State of the Global Workplace Report found that only 15% of workers were engaged in their work, and other studies, such as Deloitte's Global Human Capital Trends reports, have also pointed over the past several years to the need for a shift away from process-oriented authoritarianism and stringent control to a more person-centred, or human, approach to organisational leadership and management.

Yet we seem to find it hard to let go, perhaps because of the apparent rationality of focusing on processes and efficiency for effectiveness. And, perhaps, because many managers find it easier to control processes than to deal with the foibles of the human species!

INTRODUCTION

THE PARADOX OF BEING HUMAN

The human species is a paradox. We can show great kindness and great cruelty. We want independence but depend on the group. We hold human life dear, but engage in mass wars. We have great intellectual powers, yet make simplistic political, geo-political, environmental, and societal blunders.

We are part of nature, but we've come to see ourselves as separate from and above the natural world. Our hubris as a species has led us to try to dominate and override the very system or presence we depend upon for our existence, whether you call that nature, God, Allah, universal energy, or any other term.

We are only just starting to re-realise that the way we live our lives is inextricably linked to the natural world. We're beginning to understand that we depend upon, and can learn a lot from, nature and the other forms of life that inhabit this planet alongside us.

This book is a series of African animal fables. Of course, they aren't real—they're fiction—but wherever possible they are based on the general characteristics of the animals represented.

The stories are meant to be entertaining, and you can take them simply at that face-value level if you wish. But they're also designed to show how we can live well in this world being who and what we naturally are as human beings, and how we can make a difference by showing the way for others to be who and what *they* are. Because that is leadership, and this world needs leaders.

Actually, let me clarify that: The world needs *true* leaders, leaders that others follow not because they have to but because they want to, because their character calls others to follow them, because they stand for something that resonates with others, and because they can be trusted to do what needs to be done when the situation calls for it. And, importantly, because they are kind and caring. And because they trust and believe in others.

THE PHILOSOPHY OF SELF-LED LEADERSHIP

When I talk of leaders, I'm referring to leaders at all levels in any group, from those who lead only a few, or lead only in certain situations or circumstances, to the leaders of the leaders.

As we all know, there are some who think they are leaders because they are the strongest, or the loudest, or the pushiest, or the most provocative. Or just because they have a position that suggests others must obey them.

But that's not leadership, that's just being physically strong, or loud, or pushy, or provocative, or in a position of command. (And maybe a little annoying or obnoxious!) None of those things can make one a leader. You can't be a leader unless others want to follow you, and few will want to follow someone just because they are strong, or loud, or pushy, or provocative, or just because of their position or their title. A leader must show that they are worth following.

People won't trust and be inspired to follow another unless that leader has some depth of character, clear values, some self-confidence, can a share a vision for the future—for what's possible—and has the courage to stand up for what they believe in.

And others won't follow unless that leader shows that

they, as the leader, trust, listen to, and depend on others too. A leader cannot lead alone; a leader needs followers, followers who will not only follow, but who will support, and advise, and help that leader lead well, because we all need help and support from time to time.

My late mother, Jean Ann Carroll, a much loved and respected educator, once suggested to me that a good leader is one who is willing to serve. I love that definition!

A true leader is one who pulls others together for the greater good, who rallies others round a common goal, who is a catalyst for a belief, a catalyst for action, a catalyst to make things happen. They're someone who wants to help make things better.

But those who become genuine leaders must first understand themselves, where they're strong and where they're not so strong, what they're good at and what doesn't come so naturally to them. No-one can know everything or be good at everything. Good leaders surround themselves with others in a group, so their various strengths complement each other. And a good leader knows they're not the right person to lead in every situation, so they know when to lead and when to follow.

Good leaders know what they stand for, what they believe in. They have a vision for how things could be, and they're prepared to stand up for it, to rally others round it, to help others, to guide others, to coach others, and to serve others in order to get it.

They are what I call "Self-Led Leaders".

Importantly, a Self-Led Leader helps others become Self-Led Leaders, too. They help others understand themselves better, help others become their best selves, help others live their best lives, because a Self-Led Leader knows that developing more Self-Led Leaders, all striving for the same vision of how things could be, is the best way to achieve it. As Mahatma Gandhi reputedly said, "A sign of a good leader is not how many followers you have but how many leaders you create."

HOW THIS BOOK WORKS

These fables I want to tell you embody particular aspects of the philosophy of leadership I've just explained. Each one revolves around a different element of leadership, from the underlying principles of true leadership, to self-leadership, to team building, to creating an engaged culture, to leading through ever-pervasive change, to the critical issue of effective communication.

Scattered through each fable are a number of principles that apply to the particular theme of that fable. At the end of each fable is a list of those principles to make it easier for you, if you so choose, to decipher and understand the main messages behind the story.

I hope you find these stories useful for your work and your life in general. Mostly, though, I hope you enjoy them.

HOW THE LION LEARNED TO LEAD

The Philosophy of Self-Led Leadership

HOW THE LION LEARNED TO LEAD

In the long, long ago, before Africa had drifted away from the rest of Gondwana to be Africa all on its own, the lions roamed the centre of the south of that great, exotic land where it rolled in a golden wave to the distant horizon, specked here and there with acacia and baobab and jackalberry trees.

Great herds of all manner of grazing creatures, large and small—antelopes, and zebras, and buffalos, and giraffes, and warthogs—fed on the grasses and trees of those delicious plains. And the lions fed on the grazers, because that is the order of things.

The lions were the most powerful of all the hunters, but back in those exclusive times, each lion hunted alone; they didn't share their meals, and each of them took care of themselves. And because they hunted alone, they fed almost exclusively on the smaller grazers, the abundant impala, and the wildebeest, and the warthog. It was difficult and dangerous for a single lion to try to bring down a large grazer like an eland or a buffalo.

The cunning hyenas lived to the east, in the rocky

foothills of the great range that separates the savannah from the sea. The lions had driven them there several generations before, to those granite hills, where the pickings were scarce, and only rock rabbits and baboons and lizards were abundant.

But the hyenas were strong and fearsome, with their thickset necks, and sloping backs, and powerful jaws. They could hunt and they could fight, and they had devious minds and long memories. They would make forays into the lions' territory to steal the food from under the nose of an unvigilant lion if they could. And they were always plotting ways to regain a pawhold on the abundant grasslands from which the lions had forced them.

Now, even creatures like the lions who hunted and fed on their lonesomes needed a social order. So the lions had a leader to keep the order among them, and to protect the golden grassland territory on which they all depended.

In the time of this tale, the king of the lions was a big and fearsome warrior called Shinga (which means *brave*). Shinga was acknowledged as a powerful leader because he was the bravest and the biggest, and because everyone knew he was born to be their leader. He roared like a leader, and he looked like a leader, with his black mane, and his rippling muscles, and his fierce warrior eyes.

And the other lions feared Shinga, as their parents had feared Shinga's father before him. Shinga came from a long line of strong lions, who had always kept the order of things in strict regulation, and had protected the kingdom from their bitter enemy, the hyenas.

Now, as time went by, Shinga began to grow older and weaker. And when he was finding it harder to catch anything bigger than a scrub hare to eat—remember, in those far-off days each lion hunted alone—he knew it was nearly time for his first-born son, Husimba, to take over as leader of the lions, because that was the order of things. And that worried Shinga.

Now, Husimba means *strength*, and when you think of a lion king, that's probably what you would think of—a big, strong lion like Shinga, with a fearsome roar, and rippling muscles, and a thick, dark mane, and fierce warrior's eyes.

But Husimba wasn't like that. Like all male lions, he was quite big and strong, but his roar wasn't that fearsome, and his eyes weren't the eyes of a fierce warrior.

Husimba had warm, friendly eyes. Kind eyes. And he was softly spoken, and he liked to sit under the shade of an acacia tree, out of the hot summer sun, and think.

"He worries me," Shinga said to Husimba's mother, Tira. "He is too soft, too gentle. To be the leader of the lions as is his destiny, he must be strong and forceful. Our enemies will not fear him, and the other lions will not follow him if he speaks softly and doesn't prove his strength as a warrior."

"He's still young," said Tira. "His character will grow and develop. But remember, he's not like you, Shinga. Yes, he has a kinder nature. But that doesn't make him weak."

"Nonsense!" replied Shinga. "There's no room for kindness when you're leading and protecting a kingdom. Others will take advantage of kindness. It *is* a weakness. And the king must be strong to defeat our enemies."

"I know you are strong in that way, Shinga," replied Tira

cautiously. "I have seen you use your power to discipline a lion who doesn't behave as they should. I remember how you drove Kuba from the pride after he turned on you, as I know you had to do. But there are different ways of achieving the same end. Perhaps Husimba needs to learn to be stronger in situations like that, but that doesn't mean he must become unkind. He could stand up for what he believes in, and do what he needs to do, without making others feel small or worthless."

"You see fit to contradict me, to tell me how a king should act!" snapped Shinga. "I am a strong king and that makes me a good king! I know how things must be done. And kindness has no place in that."

Now Tira was wise, and she knew not to challenge Shinga too far. So she lowered her eyes and fell silent, for that was the order of things.

But in her heart Tira knew Shinga was wrong. She was sure that Husimba could be a strong leader despite being gentle and kind; perhaps a better leader *because* he was gentle and kind.

As the unofficial leader of the lionesses, she had watched the pride and its members for many years, and she was sure that kindness had a key role to play in its leadership.

While she knew that Shinga always believed he was acting in the best interests of the pride—and she respected him for that—she had seen how the others reacted to his forceful domination, usually with obedience, but almost always with fear and often with resentment. If there was a genuine challenge for the leadership, she wondered how many of the pride would back Shinga.

We can show our anger or our disappointment when

another does wrong, she thought, *but when we're unkind, when we humiliate or disparage another, they'll most likely become defensive. Then their thoughts will probably go to their dislike of us, rather than to an acceptance and understanding of what they've done wrong. And they'll learn nothing from the experience.*

The role of the pride's leader, Tira believed, included being a teacher, a guide, and a mentor. And surely no-one would want to learn from someone who was unkind?

No, she thought. *It's better for a leader to be kind even when they have to be tough.*

Late one day, a few weeks later, Shinga summoned Husimba to join him as he sat in the falling light on the top rock of the central outcrop, surveying his territory with proud eyes.

"You were born to be leader of the lions, Husimba," Shinga said. "It is your destiny, and it will soon be your time. I know that your body is strong, but I am worried that your nature is weak. I must know that is not the case, that you can be strong in character. You must begin to give orders, to let the others know that you have power. Your roar must echo across the plains! If anyone challenges you, you must fight them and win. You must start to show that you are to be obeyed without question. Then the others will respect you and follow you when the time comes."

"Yes, father," replied Husimba. "But I am still young, and I am not yet experienced in the way of things. And many of the others are strong and brave. And of those who are not as big and strong, many are quick and agile and clever. Many are more experienced than me. When I am king, should I not seek their help and their advice?"

"No!" snarled Shinga. "You are showing your weakness! When you are king, the others will expect you to be strong, decisive, dominant. You cannot be soft. Our sworn enemy, the hyenas, want to drive us from these lands. If you do not control and lead the pride with authority and strength from the front, they will succeed. And you will have banished us to the rocky foothills. You will have failed our forefathers and failed the pride. Is that what you want as your legacy?"

"No, father." Husimba hung his head.

"Then show me that your character is strong!" And, with a searing glance, Shinga turned, leapt down from the outcrop and stalked away through the tall grass.

Husimba sat there for a long time. Stars flickered out in the darkening sky, but he barely saw them. His mind was churning. He hadn't asked to be leader of the lions. It was being thrust on him because of who his ancestors were. He wasn't sure he wanted it. What if his father was right, if he was too weak? If it took dominance and force to be a leader, he didn't know if he wanted to be that sort of lion.

But what if… the thought emerged in his mind, *…what if there's a better way to lead than Father's way?*

He instantly felt ashamed. He knew he should respect his father.

But his mind kept coming back to the same thing: he wasn't sure the pride responded well to being dominated or driven by fear. He'd seen fear act as a powerful motivator for the members of the pride, of course, but he wondered if it could also be counter-productive?

Surely, he mused, *we work best together when we're motivated by trying to achieve something together, something that's meaningful to us all. When we're driven by fear,* he reasoned, *we will often act in our own best interests to avoid the threat, perhaps at the expense of the goal.*

And perhaps worse than that, he reflected, *when we're pushed around, when we're belittled, or made to feel worthless, or criticised too often, we start to lose confidence in our own ability.*

He had seen it happen. And he'd seen how an individual's lack of confidence had affected the whole pride when they had needed to work together to defend against the hyenas.

If I am to be leader of the lions, he thought, *I would prefer to support and steer them, not to dictate and dominate them.*

But again, he felt guilty about his disloyal thoughts. And what if he was wrong? He had no real experience in these things. What if his father was right, and it *did* take force to be a good leader? But how could he fulfil his destiny when it would mean going against his true nature? Perhaps he was too weak to be king after all.

A soft voice startled him. He hadn't heard his mother approaching.

"What's troubling you, Husimba?" she asked gently.

"I don't know what to do, mother. Father wants me to become stronger in spirit, more forceful, so he can trust me to take over leadership of the pride. But I don't know if I'm capable of doing that." He hung his head. "I don't think I'm made to be a leader."

"But you *are* a leader," said Tira. "You're already strong

in spirit. Not in the same way as your father, but I have seen it many times in your heart. You just need to find trust in yourself, to understand your strengths, understand who you are as a lion. Your father believes in his own way of leading, but there are many ways to lead and many forms of strength. Force is not always the right way."

"But I'm not even a very good hunter," said Husimba. "I miss more than I succeed. I have watched you hunting, and you are far better than me."

Tira smiled. "It is the same with your father, though he would never admit it. Most male lions are not such good hunters. You are big and strong and can bring down a buffalo. But your size can also be a hindrance. We females are smaller and leaner. We're faster and more agile. We can turn and twist in the chase. That is our strength. It's not yours. But always remember, you have your own unique strengths, and they're different to your father's strengths."

She paused, then continued quietly. "Husimba, a leader must understand that we all have different strengths—where one of us is less strong in an ability or character trait, another is stronger. No-one can be strong in everything.

"So a good leader should focus on each individual's strengths, not their weaknesses. As a group, we are stronger precisely *because* we have different strengths. When we work together as a team, we depend on one another's strengths, and we can support each other to work effectively.

"Husimba, you must know and use your own strengths alongside the strengths of others in the group. When you can do that, my son, you will become a great leader."

That night, in the shadow of a ragged cliff in the rocky foothills of the great range that separates the savannah from the sea, the matriarch leader of the hyenas, Tyisa, the largest and boldest and most cunning of them all, was speaking to the clan:

"Shinga, the leader of the lions, is growing old and getting weak in body. Now is the time for us to make our move, to drive them out. Then we can take back our rightful place as leaders of all the savannah lands and we can eat abundantly."

"But there are more of them than there are of us," whined a young hyena. "It'll be dangerous."

"Not if we're clever," replied Tyisa. "And I am! Come closer," she whispered. "Here's my plan."

They shuffled round her and she spoke in a low voice for several minutes. The others giggled and squealed in excitement as she told them what they each needed to do.

"Now go," she said. "Fulfill your missions and soon the lionlands will be ours!"

The following night, the hyenas gathered once again around their leader. Tyisa looked round the circle.

"Have you all completed your missions?" she asked.

"Yes, Tyisa," said one. "I went out and told those gullible impalas the story you said to tell them, that the great Mystical Barking Baboon, who knows all things, has informed us that the streams and rivers in these parts will soon be drying up, and that all wise animals should immediately and without hesitation move south to the great grey-green, greasy Limpopo River, or they will die here of thirst. And already those stupid animals are on the move."

"I have told the wildebeest the same thing," said another.

"And I have told the warthogs," said a third.

And one by one, they gave their reports.

"Stupid grasseaters!" they all cackled. "They believe anything anyone tells them. And then they just follow each other like lemmings. They'd jump off a cliff if we told them to!"

Tyisa was pleased. "You have done well," she said. "The great exodus of the small grazers has begun. Soon the lions will have too little to eat. Because they hunt alone, they can't bring down the large grazers like the eland or the buffalo, but we hyenas, who hunt together in a pack… we can. The lions will have to follow the herds of small grazers to the south, and when they are gone, we will reclaim the grasslands that are rightfully ours and live like royalty off the herds of large grazers. Soon, my clan, we will take back the territory that was stolen from us all those summers ago. Soon we will rule the sweeping plains and be revered and feared, just as the lions are now."

The hyena clan whooped and cheered and giggled and squealed.

"Our own kingdom of plenty at last," they said to each other.

"I'm going to eat buffalo till I'm sick!" screeched a ragged old hag. "I loooove buffalo! I can't wait!"

"It will not be long now," said Tyisa. "We will watch the exodus from up on the cliff top, and when the time is right, we will make our move."

Late the next afternoon on the lionlands, Shinga sat on the top rock of the central outcrop and stared out over the rolling plains. He was puzzled and worried. The small grazers were leaving the grasslands, great herds moving southwards, crossing through the streams and over the curving horizon till they disappeared from sight.

He couldn't understand it. Why were they going? Even in the dry season, they never went far. When the streams stopped running, the herds could still find water in the remaining pools and could browse on the scattered patches of tufty grass while they waited for the rains to come again.

And he had started to hear rumblings from the pride. It was getting harder for them to find food. If he didn't do something soon, they would lose faith in him as their leader. He had faced nothing like this before, and for the first time, he felt undecided about what course of action to take.

There was a soft rustling in the grass behind him, and Tira appeared by his side. She looked up at him.

"You seem worried, Shinga," she said.

"I am trying to reach a decision," the lion king replied. "You can see that, for some reason, the herds of small grazers are leaving the lionlands and the pride will soon be hungry. But if we follow the herds, we will leave our territory unguarded and exposed. If we stay, our usual prey will soon be gone, and we will have to hunt the large eland, or the buffalo. That will be difficult and dangerous."

"Have you spoken to any of the others to get their opinion?" asked Tira.

"You know I cannot do that," snapped Shinga. "That would show I am unsure of myself. It would show weakness.

As king, I cannot be seen to be weak, especially at a time like this."

"What about Husimba? Have you spoken to him?"

"What would Husimba know?" retorted Shinga. "He is soft and knows little."

Tira paused before replying. "I know he is still lacking in experience, but he is wiser than you think, Shinga. And if he is to take over as king one day, would it not be good to involve him now so he can learn from you?"

Shinga stared at her hard for a moment. "Mmm…" he said at last. "He does need to learn. It may do him good to be with me at this time. Send him to me, Tira. I will talk with him."

A short time later, Husimba climbed the central outcrop and stood respectfully beside his father.

The king looked at him appraisingly. "Your mother says that though you are still young and inexperienced, you are wise. We will see. What do you make of the situation with the herds?"

"It worries me, Father," replied Husimba. "The pride is getting hungry and restless."

"I know that!" snapped Shinga. "But show me this wisdom of yours. Do you have a solution?"

Husimba hesitated. "Father, I may not be as forceful as you, but the members of the pride talk to me. I get to hear what is going on. There is bickering among them. Some are saying the herds will come back on their own because there is plentiful grass on the savannah. Others say we should follow them. Some believe there is something you are keeping from the pride. And Father…" he paused again. "I think you should know that I overheard some of the young males talking of overthrowing you as king."

"And you?" snarled the king. "What do you think about that? Do you want to overthrow me?"

"No, Father." Husimba shook his head. "I believe we all need to work together right now. But I think the pride needs guidance to keep us together."

"And just what do you suggest I do?" retorted Shinga scathingly. "If we follow the herds, we leave the lionlands unprotected. If we stay, the pride must take the risk of hunting the larger grazers or remain hungry. Whatever choice I make leaves the pride in danger."

Husimba hesitated. "I think the herds will come back," he said. "Whatever has caused them to leave, there is still good grazing for them here. There are no grasslands like this to the south where they going. But the pride must be able to eat in the meantime, and many are too fearful to take on a large animal like a buffalo."

Husimba paused again. Then he said slowly, "Perhaps there is a third alternative, Father. Mother said we all have different strengths and I've been thinking about that. What if we stayed on the lionlands, but learned to hunt together in groups instead of alone? With their speed and agility, a group of females could together run down a buffalo, or an eland, with ease. And if there were too few in the group to bring it to the ground, then a male, with his size and strength, could bring it down once the females have slowed it. A single buffalo or eland could feed at least six of us at a time if we shared the kill."

"You think the pride would be prepared to share?" retorted his father. "They have never hunted together or eaten together before. That is not the way we do things. The pride will not want to change from the ways they know."

"We could ask them," said Husimba. "If they feel they have been asked for their opinion and heard, they may be more prepared to try something new. And perhaps one of them may have a better idea."

Shinga was thoughtful for some time. Then he said in a low and measured voice, "I can see that your idea might work, Husimba. But a leader must be decisive. If I ask the pride to make the decision about what we should do, they will see me as a weak leader. My position and the position of our family line could be at risk."

"With respect, Father," replied Husimba, his confidence growing. "I understand what you're saying. But I don't believe you need to ask the pride to make the decision, just to get their input. From what I've heard, the pride wants to feel they can trust you to lead them through this uncertainty. And I think trust must be earned both ways. If you are prepared to hear their opinions and ideas, and *then* you make your decision based on your thoughts *and* their thoughts, that will show them you have confidence and trust in yourself and in them. And if they feel you trust them, they are more likely to trust you.

"If the group sees you as being both trusting and trustworthy, they may be prepared to try the new way of hunting. Then we will grow stronger than ever under your leadership because the pride will feel we can all truly work together to overcome this threat."

Shinga looking appraisingly at Husimba. Then he nodded.

"Perhaps," he said.

By the time the sun cast its first yellow glow across the land the following morning, in the rocky foothills of the great range that separates the savannah from the sea, the hyenas were getting restless too.

"The lions have not left yet, Tyisa," whined one of the males. "We want the kingdom you promised us."

"And our buffalo!" said the ragged old hag.

"What if they don't go?" asked another.

"Do you think I don't have a Plan B?" snapped the matriarch. "Plan B is 'divide and conquer'. Last night, I crept in to see what the lions were doing. Shinga saw me and tried to attack me, but he is too old and slow! And I had seen enough. There is disagreement among them. If they have not left to follow the herds by tonight, we will move in and overpower them while they are divided. And we will drive them out!"

At the same time, an unusual gathering was taking place below the central outcrop on the savannah. Shinga was addressing the pride.

"We are in an unprecedented and dangerous situation, as I'm sure you are all well aware. Yesterday I spoke with my son, and I have instructed him to speak to you now. Listen to what he has to say."

There was a murmur from the gathered lions. Shinga had never let anyone else speak at a gathering before.

Husimba stepped forward and, hesitantly at first, then with growing confidence, outlined his shared hunting and feeding idea.

"So," he concluded after a few minutes, "if you choose to follow this new way, we will all have to act together for it to work. I believe we have the strength between us to get through this situation if we work together. In fact, I believe we will come out stronger as a pride on the other side *because* we will have worked together. We will have used our combined strengths to make life better than it is now for all of us."

He glanced at his father, who sat staring straight ahead. Taking a deep breath, he continued. "Some of you may have ideas that will help this plan work better. Or perhaps you have some different ideas. We would like to hear them. What do you think?"

There was a silence. Then a hum of voices.

Then the biggest and boldest of the young males spoke up. "I am prepared to try this new way. We will hunt together and feed together. But I have a suggestion if you are truly prepared to listen?"

Shinga rose to his feet. "You ask to speak. Yet I have heard that yesterday you were planning to overthrow me. Why should I trust what you have to say?"

The young male was silent for a short while. Then he said, "I am sorry, Shinga. The situation is new and difficult, as you said. But the pride must be able to eat and we had heard nothing from you. But you have now given us a plan that could work. So I am willing to try to help if you will hear me."

Shinga stared at him. "Under the law of the lionlands, I should cast you from the pride," he said. "But I realise that your concern was for the group. So I will not do that. I would like to hear what you have to say. You may speak."

The young male bowed his head in respect. "Thank you, Shinga. I am grateful. And because of that, I will not try to challenge you for the leadership again. I give you my word. My idea is this: Since, as Husimba says, we males are stronger fighters than the females, but not as agile as hunters, I would like to take a group of us younger, stronger males to patrol the territory to protect against an attack from the hyenas, while the females, backed by the older males when needed, could hunt as a group. Then we could all take it in turns to eat, sharing the females' kill."

Tira had watched the proceedings nervously and, while she was a little surprised at the outcome, she was proud of both her son and her husband.

Well, well, she thought. *Maybe Husimba has taught Shinga something about leadership… and Shinga was prepared to learn!*

And the new hunting process they'd come up with sounded good. Perhaps now that Shinga had seen that working *with* the others, instead of simply controlling them, could produce a good result, he would continue in that way, and perhaps more good ideas would come from the pride.

Tira felt sure that if Shinga could lead by inspiring and guiding instead of through fear, just ensuring that the new hunting process was followed and maybe improved, his role as king would be so much easier.

The pride, she reflected, *will readily follow different ways of doing things if they've helped create them. And if they feel they're trusted, if they're able to work with their own strengths, they'll be much more likely to do what needs to be done under Shinga's guidance without being continually pushed.*

If that can happen, she thought hopefully, *Shinga won't feel the need to lead by fear, to constantly dominate and control. And,* she smiled to herself, *life will be better that way for all of us.*

And so it was that the lions learned to work together. The team of young males, led by the biggest and boldest, fought off the hyenas' attack, while the females led the hunt in the new system. And when the hyenas had been driven back into the rocky foothills, the lions all ate in turn together.

And over time, once the herds of smaller grazers had returned to the grasslands, the lions kept and perfected their new hunting process, and so became stronger as a group and grew in number as a pride. And when they reached the right age, some young lions, with the blessing of the king, would go off to start their own prides in other territories, taking the new ways with them.

And the hyenas? Well, they learned it was best for them if they stayed in the shadows, hunting together when the time was right, scavenging when opportunity arose, and every now and then feasting on buffalo.

And today, lions still dominate the savannah plains, working with their own strengths, and leaders in their own way, each and every one of them.

Main Messages From the Fable:

The Five Principles of Self-Led Leadership

Self-Led Leaders:

1. Are kind even when they have to be tough

2. Support and steer, don't dictate and dominate

3. Focus on strengths, not weaknesses

4. Are trusting and trustworthy

5. Lead people and manage processes

HOW THE RHINOCEROS GOT ITS SKIN

Leading Yourself So You Can Lead Others

(Loosely based on one of Rudyard Kipling's "Just So" stories)

HOW THE RHINOCEROS GOT ITS SKIN

In the long, long ago, before the what of now, a Most Powerful N'anga lived in the southern parts of the exotic and magical continent called Africa, near the great, grey-green, greasy Limpopo River, on the edge of the Altogether Uninhabited Interior.

Now, a n'anga is a very important person who can cure sick people with mysteriously concocted ingredients that most doctors from now don't know about. A 'Most Powerful' N'anga is even more special because they can cast spells on people, so their minds make strange and sensational things happen to them.

This Most Powerful N'anga lived in totally tolerable comfort in a hut made of sticks and mud on the edge of a little village. He wore a Most Wonderful Leopard Skin Hat, and the people of the village made his food for him because he was a very kind Powerful N'anga and was much too busy doing powerful things to cook for himself. (And, if the truth be told, the N'anga knew he was most definitely not powerful at cooking.)

One fine day, the people of the village took a whole field of corn and pounded it in their biggest pot until it was all ground down to powder. Then they mixed it most slowly and carefully with water until they couldn't mix it any more. And they pounded it and pushed it and jumped on it until it was flat and three arms long all the way round.

(I hope they washed their feet before jumping on it because they had no shoes in those days and their feet would have been very dirty. They must have, because it didn't seem to taint the deliciousness of the dish.)

Then the villagers covered that corn with lots of scrumptious roots and berries to make a cake, and they baked it over a fire until it was all done brown and smelt very sentimental. And they took that cake, all steamy hot, to the Most Powerful N'anga.

"Oh, thank you," said the Most Powerful N'anga. "I am lucky to live with such kind people. Won't you please join me to help eat this delectable cake?"

The Most Powerful N'anga often reflected on how lucky he was to live among the people of the village, where Ubuntu, that great philosophy of life, was their guiding principle.

"I am me because we are we," the people of the village would often say, especially when they achieved some great feat or some good fortune befell the village.

And the N'anga knew that his own power was only powerful because he was in the fortunate position of being

HOW THE RHINOCEROS GOT ITS SKIN

able to help the others. Without them, his power would be power*less*.

I am a very lucky n'anga, he sometimes reflected. *I am privileged more than powerful.*

So the villagers and the Most Powerful N'anga all sat down round the fire, but before they could start to eat, out of the Altogether Uninhabited Interior came one Rhinoceros, big and strong, with a horn on its nose, two piggy eyes, no manners whatsoever, and a tight, shiny skin of which it was excessively proud.

In those days, the Rhinoceros's skin was smooth as smooth and had no wrinkles in it anywhere. All the same, when you know a bit more about him, you'll see that didn't matter one little crease, because he had no manners, which was a very big wrinkle in that Rhinoceros. He thought that because he was bigger and stronger, he was entitled to take whatever he wanted whenever he wanted it, and that's exactly what he did. And to this day, he still doesn't have any manners, and maybe he never will.

The Rhinoceros said "Humph," and all the villagers ran screaming back to their huts in the village. The Most Powerful N'anga left his cake and immediately climbed to the top of an acacia tree.

The Rhinoceros trampled on the Most Powerful N'anga's fire to put it out just because he could and just to show that he was the boss, and then he spiked the cake on the horn of his nose.

The Most Powerful N'anga shouted at him from the

top of his acacia tree. "Iwe!" (which sort of means "Hey, you!") "Iwe! That's *our* cake! You can have some—I am happy to share—but leave some for the others and some for tomorrow."

"Humph!" replied the Rhinoceros. "Won't! I'm big and I'm strong and I'm powerful. And I'm hungry right now."

And the Rhinoceros ate that cake in one big mouthful. Then he went away, waving his tail proudly, back to the Altogether Uninhabited Interior.

The Most Powerful N'anga sat up in his tree for a long while, thinking deep thoughts about those who are inconsiderate and who put themselves first, regardless of the consequences for others. He thought about those who stamp out other people's fires, who want to pull others down to boost their own ego. And he thought about those who use their strength, or their position of power, to dominate others.

We all want to be respected, mused the N'anga. *And we all want to be liked by at least some others. But no-one likes or respects those who are inconsiderate of others. And being able to make others do things because you have power and they fear you, does not get you liked, and most certainly does not gain you respect. Both liking and respect come from* who *you are,* thought the N'anga, *not* what *you are.*

And it struck the N'anga that the Rhinoceros's behaviour had an even worse consequence: Those who are inconsiderate, he realised, or who use fear and force to dominate others will probably not even like and respect themselves very much. They will know deep down that behaving that way is not the right thing to do.

The N'anga shook his head sadly. *Those who act that way must be very uncomfortable in their own skins,* he thought. *It would be better for them if they learned to be more considerate and caring, so they could feel comfortable in themselves. Then they would be happier individuals.*

And, having thought that thought, the Most Powerful N'anga came down from his acacia tree, smiling a wry smile to himself. Then he made his fire again, and he danced around it three times, reciting the following saying:

"Them that takes cakes
And others forsakes
Makes dreadful mistakes!"

And there was a great deal more in that saying than you would think!

Now, a few weeks later there was a heat wave in the southern parts of Africa, and all the people in the village took off all the clothes they had on (in those far-off days it wasn't illegal to take off all your clothes in public because there wasn't any legal, which made it easier to do a lot of things) and they all went to swim in the great, grey-green, greasy Limpopo River, taking special care to look out for crocodiles, of course.

But the Most Powerful N'anga didn't go for a swim because he was worried that the water might wash away his magic.

Then the Rhinoceros came out of the Altogether Uninhabited Interior and also set off for the river to have a swim. But on his way, seeing the village empty, he stopped immediately and trampled out the fire outside each hut just because he could, and then he ate all the food he could find.

Well, just then, the Most Powerful N'anga happened to pass by the village, and he saw what that rhinoceros had done.

"Iwe!" he said to the Rhinoceros. "You have stamped out all the fires and eaten all the food. The villagers will have to start their fires again and they have nothing left to eat. You should think about other people, because if you don't, they won't think about you when you need them to!"

"Won't!" said the Rhinoceros. "I'm big and I'm strong and I can do what I want. And I wanted to do that!"

And he went proudly down to the river without another thought, waving his tail, and feeling even bigger and stronger, though he was quite bloated from eating so much.

The Most Powerful N'anga stared after him, shaking his head. *That Rhinoceros is completely reactive,* he thought. *He doesn't stop to think about what he is doing, about the impact on others, or the consequences for himself. He just reacts.*

But the thing is, the N'anga reflected, *we all have choices. And we always have time to think, even if it's only a very quick thought, before we react. If we don't, very often we will make a bad choice. It's much better,* thought the N'anga, *to reflect before we react.*

--- ✦ ---

But the Rhinoceros certainly wasn't reflecting. He walked straight and directly to the river, and when he got there, he took off his tight, shiny skin, of which he was excessively proud. In those days, his skin buttoned underneath with three buttons. It looked like a shiny raincoat.

And he waddled straight into the water, leaving his skin

on the river bank, and he sat there blowing bubbles through his nose.

Presently, the Most Powerful N'anga came by and found the Rhinoceros's skin. He walked slowly round that skin, thinking deep thoughts about how things would be if the villagers could just live peacefully and didn't have to worry about the Rhinoceros stamping out their fires and eating their food.

This Rhinoceros is very foolish, the N'anga thought to himself. *He just charges around doing what he wants. He doesn't think about others, and he doesn't think about the consequences for tomorrow of what he does today. He needs to learn a lesson.*

The N'anga pondered a few ponders for a bit. Then he stopped pondering, and he smiled one smile that ran all round his face two times.

And he danced three times round the skin, rubbing his hands. (The Rhinoceros didn't see the N'anga dancing round his skin, probably because rhinoceroses don't have very good eyesight.)

And the Most Powerful N'anga went to his hut, and he filled his Most Wonderful Leopard Skin Hat with corn-cake crumbs, for that N'anga only ate corn-cake, and he never swept out his hut. (In the day and age of now, his hut would have been infested with cockroaches, but back then, cockroaches hadn't been invented yet in that part of the world.)

Then the Most Powerful N'anga took that Rhinoceros's skin, and he shook that skin, and he scrubbed that skin, and he rubbed that skin just as full of old, dry, stale, tickly corn-cake crumbs as ever it could possibly hold.

And he danced three times round the skin, reciting his Most Powerful Saying again, only this time just a little bit different to add to the power:

"Them that takes cakes
And tomorrow forsakes
Makes dreadful mistakes!"

And that was a very powerful saying indeed, especially when it was combined with the N'anga's first saying a few pages ago!

We all need to have values to guide how we live today, thought the N'anga, *so we can live well today, and our tomorrow will be the way we'd like it to be. If we want food tomorrow, we must plant crops today. And if we want to have friends who care about us tomorrow, we must build friendships today. But that Rhinoceros doesn't seem to care! And he'll be a very unhappy and uncomfortable Rhinoceros tomorrow if he doesn't change his ways today.*

Vision and values, thought the N'anga. *Yes, that's a good way to see it. We should all have a vision and values. Vision and values help us to be comfortable with ourselves, comfortable in our own skins. They help to guide us so we can be the sort of person we need to be to live the sort of life we want to live now and tomorrow. I hope the Rhinoceros can learn that,* he thought.

Having thought those powerful thoughts, the N'anga shook out a few corn-cake crumbs that had got stuck in his Most Wonderful Leopard Skin Hat, and put his hat back on his head. Then he climbed to the top of his acacia tree and waited for the Rhinoceros to come out of the water and put his skin back on.

And at last the Rhinoceros did. He buttoned his skin up with the three buttons, and it tickled like cake crumbs in bed. Then he wanted to scratch, but that made it worse. So he lay down in the sand and rolled, and rolled, and rolled, but every time he rolled the cake crumbs tickled him worse, and worse, and worse.

Then he ran to the acacia tree and rubbed, and rubbed, and rubbed himself against it. He rubbed so much and so hard that he rubbed his skin until it folded over his legs, and it folded round his neck, and it got all wrinkled and crinkled. And he rubbed the buttons right off from under him. And all that rubbing nearly knocked the Most Powerful N'anga out of his acacia tree! But it didn't help the Rhinoceros's itching and scratching.

Well, all the scratching and the itching spoiled that Rhinoceros's temper, but it didn't make the least difference to the corn-cake crumbs. They were inside his skin. And he couldn't take his skin off because it didn't have buttons any more.

"Iwe!" shouted the N'anga from the top of the tree. "I can help you with that scratchy skin if you promise to start thinking about others, and to stop putting out the villagers' fires and eating their food. Maybe they'll be happy to share their food with you if you show you care about them. If you will do that, I can fix your itchy skin."

"Won't!" said the Rhinoceros. "I'm big and I'm strong and I'm the boss."

"I am very sorry you feel that way," the N'anga replied,

shaking his head sadly. "But come and see me if you decide to change."

"Won't!" said the Rhinoceros. And he turned on his tail and stomped away back home to the Altogether Uninhabited Interior, very grumpy indeed and horribly scratchy.

The Most Powerful N'anga came down from his acacia tree and lit his fire, still shaking his head and thinking sad thoughts about the foolishness of that Rhinoceros.

Well, the Rhinoceros never did decide to change. And he mostly stayed on his lonesome in the middle of the Altogether Uninhabited Interior.

And from that day to this, every rhinoceros still has great folds in their skin. And they mostly live alone because they have very bad tempers, all on account of the corn-cake crumbs making them very uncomfortable in their own skins.

So now, as the Most Powerful N'anga teaches all the young villagers, if you see someone who is very grumpy and uncaring, who tries to control everyone else to get everything their own way, perhaps it's because they're not really, truly comfortable in their own skin either.

Maybe, if they want a good today and an even better tomorrow, they need to learn to be kind to others, not to stamp out other peoples' fires, and to understand that there's enough cake for us all if we have manners and we're happy to share.

That, says the N'anga, is what makes living in our skin really and truly comfortable—putting kindness before control.

Main Messages From the Fable:

The Five Practices of Self-Led Leaders

Self-Led Leaders:

1. Feel privileged, not powerful

2. Choose to be considerate and caring

3. Reflect before they react

4. Live by a clear vision and values

5. Put kindness before control

HOW THE MEERKATS FORMED A FAMILY

Leading For a High-Functioning Team

HOW THE MEERKATS FORMED A FAMILY

IN THE LONG, LONG AGO, soon after Africa had drifted away from the rest of Gondwana to be Africa all on its own, all the meerkats lived in solitary sets of burrows on the scrubby fringe of the great Kalahari Desert in Southern Africa. In those exotic times, most meerkats were mean, miserly creatures, with greedy eyes and pointy teeth. They fought a lot because they were always trying to raid each other's burrows to get at the secret stores of delicious dried insects and scorpions that they all stashed away for a rainy day.

But there was one meerkat who was the meanest and most miserly of them all. His name was Mr Meager. He had the greediest eyes, and the pointiest teeth, and really bad breath. And he was their chief.

Mr Meager lived alone, away from everyone else, on the scrubby slopes of a yellow grass bank above a dry riverbed. The riverbed was dry because even when the rains fell in the wet season, it would simply drain away through the dusty soil of the semi-desert.

Mr Meager seldom mixed with the other meerkats, and he wouldn't let any of them near his grassy bank. Every day, he would forage systematically along his bank, first along to the left, then to the right, working his way upwards to the top, crunching and munching on beetles, and bugs, and lizards, and scorpions. And he always carefully folded some insects up in a large leaf he carried so he could hoard them away in his secret storeroom when he got home. And if another meerkat dared show its face over the top of the grassy bank, Mr Meager would dart at it savagely, squealing fiercely and shouting, "MY bank! MY beetles! MY bugs! I'm the chief! Clear off!"

Only one meerkat was ever brave enough to go near Mr Meager's grassy bank. Suri was different to the other meerkats. She was a kind, friendly young creature. She lived with her mother and two baby brothers in a cosy burrow near the big, abandoned termite mound.

Suri felt sorry for Mr Meager. She thought he must be lonely living all by himself with no-one to talk to. She'd often sneak off to watch him hunting, peeping curiously over the top of the bank. Sometimes he'd see her and chase her away, but she wasn't really afraid of him, and she'd soon be back.

In fact, Suri felt sorry for a lot of the other meerkats. She would often give insects she caught to one of the older meerkats who found it harder to catch things now they couldn't move as fast as they used to. They'd snatch it from her and gobble it down without even a thank you.

"What a stupid girl, giving away your food! But I'll have it if you don't want it," they'd cackle.

But Suri just went on giving them things. Her mother would shake her head and smile.

"My Suri's a little different," she'd say to Suri's aunt. "She's a dreamer. I don't know where she gets it from. She's always saying that if we all helped each other, everyone would be better off. Once she even asked me why we don't share burrows we can all bolt down together if there's danger while we're out foraging."

"Fancy that!" Suri's aunt would reply. "Imagine being in a burrow with Mr Meager!" And they'd both laugh.

But behind it all, her mother was very proud of Suri. She was proud of Suri's kindness. She was proud of Suri's philosophy that sharing would make things better for everyone.

My Suri is very clear about what she wants to do, she thought. *She knows how she wants to help the meerkat mob—she's got such a strong sense of purpose. She's a meerkat on a mission!*

One morning at the beginning of a strange, wet summer, just as Mr Meager was about to come out of his burrow, he heard a sort of rushing sound, and the ground went a bit shivery like hundreds of animals stampeding closer.

"I'm being attacked!" thought Mr Meager. "They want my food store! I'll show them what for!"

And he rushed out of his burrow and up the bank,

squealing and yelling: "MY bank! MY beetles! MY bugs! I'm the chief! Clear off!"

But there was no-one there. Not a soul. Mr Meager stopped near the top of the bank and sat up, looking around, puzzled. The rushing sound was getting louder. He'd never heard anything like it.

Below him, the riverbed was a slow trickle of water, which was unusual. The early rains had been heavy that season, heavier than anyone could remember.

Suddenly, the rushing sound grew to a deafening roar and round the bend in the riverbed came a churning wall of muddy water. In seconds it was swirling round Mr Meager's legs, knocking him over and sweeping him away.

The next thing he knew, Mr Meager was a bedraggled ball, caught in the low fork of a tree where the surging water had tossed him. He looked around, confused. Where was he? He seemed to be on the banks of a fast-flowing, muddy river. Then he realised—the fast-flowing river was where his home had been. The water was right up to the base of the old camelthorn tree that stood above his burrow!

"My home! My food store!" thought Mr Meager, horrified.

He climbed down from the tree carefully and sat on top of the bank, looking dejectedly at the water churning branches, and sticks, and debris past where his home had been. He shivered. He hated being wet. All meerkats do.

"Oh, dear!" said a voice behind him. "Poor Mr Meager."

Mr Meager leapt round. A small young meerkat stood there, staring at the swirling water.

"Clear off!" snapped Mr Meager.

The young meerkat shook her head sadly.

"But your home… Whatever are you going to do? Poor Mr Meager."

"Clear off!" said Mr Meager again. "And I'm not poor! I'm the chief. And I have a very large store of… of…" His voice trailed away as he realised that he didn't. He didn't have anything anymore.

"And you're all wet," said the young meerkat. "You must be very uncomfortable. I know. You'll have to come home with me and get dry and warm. My mother won't mind."

"Clear off," said Mr Meager again, a little less forcefully this time.

"I'm Suri," said the young meerkat, undaunted.

"I don't care who you are," growled Mr Meager. "I can look after myself. Clear off! Leave me alone."

"But you don't have a home anymore," said Suri. "You've nowhere to hide if danger comes."

Mr Meager was quiet for a moment. He hadn't thought of that. The scrubby grassland didn't offer much shelter. And getting dry did sound tempting.

"I'll dig another home," he mumbled. "Go away!"

As he spoke, a movement in the nearby scrub caught his eye. Something long. Something smooth and slidy.

"Ssso," said a sleek voice. "What have we here?"

A mottled triangular head poked out of the scrub and peered at the two meerkats. Then a long, patterned body began to appear… It appeared, and appeared, and appeared.

The African Rock Python sniffed around Suri and Mr Meager with its forked tongue.

"Lost, are we?" he said.

"N…No," stuttered Suri. Although she'd heard of him,

she had never seen the African Rock Python before. "Mr Meager's home's been flooded."

"Ssso sssad," said the python. "Sssame as mine. Sssuch a ssstorm upssstream. Ssswept me away."

He circled the two meerkats slowly.

"Sssuch hard work ssswimming for ssso long in that ssstrong water. I'm ssstarving," he whispered. And his tongue flickered measuringly at Suri and Mr Meager.

Suri swallowed hard. "I…I think he wants to eat us! Run, Mr Meager! This way!"

Mr Meager looked at her, then back at the snake. And the two meerkats turned and scampered away as fast as they could.

"Ssstop," said the python, slithering after them. "I just want to talk to you."

"Down here!" Suri shot into a hole behind a small corkwood tree, Mr Meager right behind her.

"Follow me," panted Suri, and she led Mr Meager through a maze of tunnels until, at last, they came out into a small open room.

"Here we are. My home," she said.

Mr Meager looked around. "Not very big," he complained.

"You can stay with us until the water goes down and you can get back into your own burrow," said Suri. "I'm sure my mother won't mind."

"Mmh," grunted Mr Meager. "I suppose it'll have to do."

For all his bluster and bad manners, Mr Meager was rather impressed by Suri. Her quick thinking had saved the day. Saved his life, probably. And she seemed so self-assured, so comfortable in herself.

She's different, this young meerkat, he thought. *She takes the initiative herself. And she seems to genuinely care about me and the others. If only the other meerkats were like that,* he thought. *How much easier my job as Chief would be if they were all so self-sufficient. None of them will do anything except find their own food and eat it unless I tell them what to do. It's so tiresome trying to get them to work together and co-operate without hours of complaining and squabbling over petty issues.*

I wonder if they could learn to organise themselves, he pondered. *If only…*

Suri's voice dragged Mr Meager's thoughts back to the burrow.

"We'll be safe here," Suri was saying. "The Rock Python won't find us through all our tunnels."

But even as Suri spoke, slowly and surely, the python's forked tongue was following their scent through the burrowed earth. He inched forward, flicking his tongue this way and that at each fork and each cross tunnel.

At last, he heard voices ahead of him. He stopped and listened.

"I think we should all help each other more," Suri was saying to Mr Meager. "We're all good at something, different things. You're good at hunting, Mr Meager. And at coming up with systems. I've seen the way you hunt—it's very methodical. Zig zagging across your grassy bank.

"And my mum's good at caring for pups. She's ever so good with my two baby brothers. And some of the others are good at digging burrows, and some are better than others at catching scorpions. I've been watching them all. It's very interesting! And just imagine, Mr Meager, if we could all get to know what each of us is good at, and if we all helped each other with the things we're best at. Wouldn't it make things so much easier?

"And it'd be so much better if we all shared our food instead of trying to steal each other's all the time. Here, have a scorpion, Mr Meager—they're delicious."

The python was gliding silently forward again. It wasn't easy in the narrow tunnels, and it was some time before his head inched round the last bend. He stopped, flickering his tongue in and out in anticipation.

"Ssso, this is where you got to," said the snake. "Just as we were getting to know each other."

Mr Meager almost choked on the scorpion. He jumped back, his coat bristling.

"Well we don't want to get to know you," he growled at the python.

And, darting forward, he nipped the snake on the nose. It hissed in pain.

"Well done, Mr Meager!" exclaimed Suri and together the two meerkats circled in front of the snake's head, just out of reach, darting in and nipping him every time he tried to move forward.

The python tried to pull his head back. But he couldn't. The tunnel was too narrow. He slid forward again. Both meerkats nipped him at the same time.

And every time he moved, he got a nip on the nose until at last he realised he was beaten. "Alright," he pleaded. "Stop! I give up. But I can't turn round in this tunnel. Let me come out and I won't hurt you."

"If we let you come out," said Mr Meager, giving him a little nip for good measure, "do you promise to go back to your home and never to come here again?"

"Yes, yes!" moaned the snake. "Anything! Just stop biting me!"

"I don't trust him," whispered Suri.

"Me neither," Mr Meager replied. "But he's too big. We'll never get him out on our own, and you don't want a huge snake stuck in your burrow! But he can't move fast in there. If we run for it, we can be out before he slides free."

They turned and darted up the main burrow entrance into the fresh air. Suri's mother was just coming home with her two little brothers. Suri told her what had happened.

"Your daughter saved me," Mr Meager said to Suri's mother. "That python would have eaten me if she hadn't led me into your home." He stopped, embarrassed. "I'm… Well, I'm… I'm ever so grateful."

Suri's mother looked at Mr Meager in surprise. It was the first time she'd ever heard him say anything nice.

"Mr Meager was ever so brave," said Suri. "He bit the python right on the nose when it first tried to come into our living room!"

Mr Meager looked embarrassed.

"Well," said Suri's mother slowly. "It sounds like you've saved each other."

"But the python's still down there." Mr Meager pointed to the burrow.

Suri looked thoughtful. "I've got an idea," she said. "If we get everyone together, maybe we can chase him away when he comes out."

Mr Meager looked doubtful. Would that work? Would

they be able to scare the python off? It was so big. And would the others co-operate? It could be dangerous. They'd probably just argue and bicker. But, Mr Meager realised, he didn't have a better idea. And this young Suri seemed to be good with ideas. And she seemed to be good at getting others to co-operate.

He nodded. "Alright. It's worth a try. I'll call an emergency meeting. With all of us together maybe we can scare him so much he'll never come back."

It was some time later that the African Rock Python slid up and out of the burrow. He stopped and peered around. In front of him was a great mass of furry animals, hair bristling, backs arched, all growling, and barking, and hissing at him.

Mr Meager stepped forward. "Go away like you promised," he said. "And if you ever come back, remember how many of us there are. We stick together, and we've got a lot of teeth between us!"

And for good measure, all the meerkats rushed at the snake together, teeth bared. He turned tail and slithered away as fast as his scales could carry him.

"Well," said Mr Meager when the cheering died down. "He's gone. But I still don't trust him, so we need to keep an eye out. And since young Suri here has shown me how much better it is if we work together and help each other, I'll take first watch."

And without another word, Mr Meager climbed onto a tall anthill, and sat up on his hind legs, his eyes scanning the scrubby bush. The others stood staring at him in amazement.

"What are you waiting for?" he grumbled. "Go and find food. I'll stay here on watch, and I'll call out if I see danger. But we've got to take turns. We've all got to eat, remember. So one of you can come and take over a bit later."

We have to learn to trust each other, thought Mr Meager. *I must show them they can trust me first,* he thought. *I'm the Chief. If they can't trust me while I'm on watch, this won't work at all. And I'll have to trust them when they're on watch.*

"And when you're on duty," he admonished, "make sure you call out regularly, so we know you're still here and haven't fallen asleep!"

It may take some time, he thought, *but if we can learn to do that, to trust each other... well, the possibilities are enormous!* He felt quite excited at the prospect. It was a very long time since he'd felt so positive. It was a good feeling.

Mr Meager sat up on the anthill for an hour. Every now and then he'd give a quick chirrup to let the others know he was still there, still watching. When his tummy started grumbling, Suri took his place. Then, one of the others took her place.

And so it went on all day and in the days that followed. The stealing and squabbling soon stopped because the meerkats found they didn't need to hoard food; they could eat well through the day, foraging safely together, with one always on watch.

The African Rock Python never came back. And over time, the meerkats learned to really trust each other, and they found that when they worked together, things were much better for them all.

From that small beginning, meerkats have come to depend on each other, to care for one another, and to be kinder to each other. And to this day, they still take turns to keep watch, barking a warning when danger looms so they can all dive for the nearest burrow.

And now they live as a real community, one big family working together as a team, digging burrows together, feeding together, sharing the babysitting of their pups, and caring for one another.

And that's why meerkats thrive in the harsh semi-deserts of Southern Africa. Life is better for us all if we work together and are kind to one another.

And the African Rock Python? Well, he's still alone. And he's an endangered species.

Main Messages From the Fable:

> ## The Five Principles of High-Functioning Teams
>
> ### A High-Functioning Team:
>
> 1. Knows its purpose and fit
>
> 2. Is self-managed
>
> 3. Understands and respects each team member's strengths
>
> 4. Shows two-way trust
>
> 5. Shows kindness and caring

HOW THE ELEPHANT GOT ITS TRUNK

Leading For an Engaged Culture

(Loosely based on one of Rudyard Kipling's "Just So" Stories)

HOW THE ELEPHANT GOT ITS TRUNK

IN THE LONG, LONG AGO, before Africa had drifted away from the rest of Gondwana to be Africa all on its own, the elephants all lived together in the southern-most parts of that great and exotic land. And none of them had a trunk. They had a short, bulgy little nose that they could wriggle about, but they couldn't squirt water, or wave it about, or pick anything up with it.

Those were fat, easy times, and elephants back then were very uninquisitive creatures. None of them had any idea of a why or a purpose. They just followed each other about, browsing on grass, chatting round the water hole, and resting in the shade of acacia trees, not thinking about much at all except where to get the tastiest grass.

But there was one elephant, a new elephant, an Elephant's Child, who was filled with what Rudyard Kipling called ''satiable curtiosity'.

This Elephant's Child was a very courteous, polite child,

but she was also very curious. She didn't like just following everyone else, so she was always asking questions.

The Elephant's Child asked her mother, (most politely), why elephants have such big ears and she asked her broad aunt, the hippopotamus, why hippos have red sweat (they do!) and she asked her tall uncle, the ostrich, why ostriches eat stones (which is also true!), and the answer was always the same: that's the way it had always been, and stop bothering them, and just eat some grass.

And still the Elephant's Child was full of 'satiable curtiosity, and she grew more and more bored, and more and more frustrated, because no-one would answer her questions.

This is pointless, she often thought. *There's no purpose to it. I don't want to just stand around eating grass. There's more to everything than that! I have things I want to know, things I want to explore, things I want to do.*

One hot day, the Elephant's Child thought of a new question she had never asked before.

She asked, "What does the Crocodile have for dinner?"

Her mother and her aunts and uncles were horrified! "Shhh!" they whispered. "Don't ask such questions! Just eat your grass." And they all looked around fearfully, as if the Crocodile might suddenly appear.

Well, the Crocodile didn't appear, though the Elephant's Child wished it would because she had never seen a crocodile and she very much wanted to.

After asking for the tenth time what the Crocodile had

for dinner and, for the tenth time getting the same fearful "shhhh!" in reply and being told for the umpteenth time to stop asking questions and to just eat her grass, the Elephant's Child was very frustrated.

They don't understand, she thought. *These questions are important, and I'm good at questions. But they don't listen to me. They think I'm just a silly child. I can't just stand around all day eating grass. I have to find answers.*

And she made a decisive decision. She decided to run away to find an answer to her newest curtious question.

So the Elephant's Child set off on her curtious adventure to find out what the Crocodile had for dinner.

She came across the aristocratic-looking Secretary Bird, striding around on her long, bare legs, stirring up the grass to catch lizards, and mice, and insects.

"'Scuse me," said the Elephant's Child most politely. "I've asked my mother and my aunts and uncles lots and lots of questions, but they're too busy just eating grass to answer me. And I want to know what the Crocodile has for dinner."

"If you have a question," said the Secretary Bird, ruffling out the quilled feathers on her head and looking down her aristocratic beak, "and no-one answers it, find out the answer for yourself. But you must know what you're good at before you can know how to find those answers. What *are* you good at, Elephant's Child? What are your strengths?"

"Well," pondered the Elephant's Child, "I'm good at asking questions... Oh, and I don't give up. I'm very persistent!"

"So," said the Secretary Bird, "you're good at asking questions and wanting to find the answers. You must use those strengths. You must satisfy your continual curiosity. So, Elephant's Child, if you have a high risk appetite, go to the banks of the great, grey-green, greasy Limpopo River, all set about with fever trees, and there you may discover what the Crocodile has for dinner."

Well, the Elephant's Child didn't know what a risk appetite was, but she knew she was very hungry for an answer to her question. So she set off to find the great, grey-green, greasy Limpopo River, all set about with fever trees.

She walked south through the dry and dusty Lowveld, all scattered with baobab trees. And she got a bit sunburnt because baobab trees grow upside down and don't give much shade.

And she got covered in flies which tickled her sunburned skin and were very annoying. But she walked on and on until at last she came to a long curvy line of fever trees and there was the great, grey-green, greasy Limpopo River.

The first thing she saw was the wise old Chacma Baboon sitting in the sun on a tree stump.

"'Scuse me," said the Elephant's Child most politely. "But would you know where I could find the Crocodile in these promiscuous parts?"

The Baboon looked at her with his mystical head on one side.

"The Crocodile is nowhere and he's everywhere," replied the Chacma Baboon. "If you look for him, sometimes you can't see him. But he can see you. Tell me, Elephant's Child, why do you want to find the Crocodile?"

"I want to know what he has for dinner," said the

Elephant's Child. "My family won't help me find the answer. I've asked them lots and lots of curious questions and they always tell me to just be quiet and eat my grass. But I can't do that. I can't just follow them around. I've got questions to ask, answers to find, things to know."

"Oh-hoh!" said the Baboon. "I see! You want knowledge? You want to stretch your mind? That is very good. Because if you stretch your mind, you can stretch your whole world."

This Elephant's Child is wise for her age, thought the Baboon. *Her family does not understand how important her curiosity is. She will learn and grow while they will continue to just follow each other around to find the tastiest grass. And when problems arise, they won't know how to find answers. They should encourage her curiosity, not try to make her conform.*

"So, Elephant's Child," he said, "the Crocodile eats from the banks of the river. That is where you will find the answer to your curtious question."

The Elephant's Child thanked the Baboon most politely and walked on. She had gone only a little way when she trod on a log lying half in and half out of the water.

Well… she thought it was a log. But it grunted, and it winked one eye in a slow, sliding sort of way.

"'Scuse me," said the Elephant's Child most politely, stepping back off the log. "But would you know where I could find the Crocodile in these promiscuous parts?"

Then the log winked its other eye, and swirled its tail a bit in the great, grey-green, greasy water.

"Oh, yeah," said the Crocodile. "Come closer, little one, and I'll whisper it to you."

The Elephant's Child put her head down close to the Crocodile's tusky, musky mouth and the Crocodile, with a flick of his great scaly head, caught the Elephant's Child by her bulgy little nose.

"I think," said the Crocodile, "I think today I'll start with Elephant's Child!"

"Led go!" said the Elephant's Child. "You're hurtig be."

Observing all this, the old Chacma Baboon came down from his tree stump and sat on the bank above.

"I see you've found the Crocodile, oh, curious Elephant's Child. Or rather, he has found you." The Baboon chuckled a knowing chuckle. "Heh, heh! Pull. Pull hard, Elephant's Child, otherwise your new friend there in the large leather-patterned onesie will have you in that great, grey-green, greasy water before you can say handbag. Heh, heh, heh!"

So the Elephant's Child sat back on her haunches, spread her four strong, stumpy legs and pulled, and pulled. And the Crocodile pulled and pulled back, thrashing his tail about in the water like an oar. And as she pulled, the Elephant's Child's bulgy little nose began to stretch.

But after some time, the Elephant's Child felt her strong, stumpy legs starting to slip on the muddy bank, and she said through her now not so bulgy or little nose, "This is too butch for be!"

Then the Baboon came down from the bank and wrapped his long tail round a fever tree and his dexterous arms round the Elephant's Child's back legs and said, "Let's pull together, Elephant's Child, and see what we can do against this self-propelled submarine with the armour-plated upper deck. Heh, heh!"

"Thank you," gasped the Elephant's Child. "You're bery kind."

"Well," said the old Baboon, "we must support each

other. We must work together as a team, and that's what strong teams do—they support each other."

And, he thought, *we will have to be a* very *strong team if we are to win against this leather-backed submersible tank. But if we encourage and help each other towards that goal, together we can achieve great things, even during tough times like this.*

"Now pull with me, Elephant's Child, pull!" he urged.

And for what seemed like the longest of long times, all three of them pulled as hard as they could. And with each pull, the Elephant's Child's nose stretched a little more.

But in the end, the Elephant's Child and the Baboon pulled hardest. And at last, the Crocodile let go of the Elephant's Child's nose and she sat down with a bump almost squashing the old Baboon. She thanked the Baboon again for his help.

Then, the Elephant's Child and the wise old Baboon carried out essential first aid on her poor, stretched nose, which was now nearly as long as her legs. The Baboon wrapped it in cool banana leaves, and the little elephant sat under a marula tree dangling her nose in a shallow stretch of the river. The Baboon sat at the top of the bank watching her.

"You don't have to stay with me," said the Elephant's Child, most politely. "I don't want to take up too much of your time."

"I will watch for the Crocodile," replied the Baboon. "And anyway," he continued mysteriously, "we still have things to do together. We are a team now, you know. And the most important thing for a team is to get to know each other very well. We must learn how we are different and how we are the same. We must each know what we are good at and what we are not so good at. How else can we work together than by knowing *how* to work together?"

Well, the Elephant's Child sat there for three days and three nights, waiting for her nose to shrink. But it didn't.

On the fourth day, when she and the wise old Baboon had talked enough for now, she was sitting blowing bubbles to entertain herself when a horse fly came along and bit her on the shoulder.

And before she thought what she was doing, the Elephant's Child lifted up her new, stretched nose and whacked the fly with it.

"Heh, heh!" said the Baboon. "You could not have done that with your small, bulgy nose. Now, aren't you getting hungry?"

And before she thought what she was doing, the Elephant's Child reached out with her long nose, plucked a large bundle of grass from the bank, dusted it clean against her front legs, and stuffed it in her mouth.

"Heh, heh!" said the Baboon. "You couldn't have done *that* with your small, bulgy nose. And what about those marula berries in the branches above you? They're rather good. Just ripe, but still retaining a little crunch."

And before she thought what she was doing, the Elephant's Child reached up with her nose, pulled a few berries off the tree, and tipped them into her mouth.

"Heh, heh!" said the Baboon. "You couldn't have done that with your small, bulgy nose. Isn't it amazing what a little stretching can do!"

The Elephant's Child sat thoughtfully for a while. At last she said, "I'll think I'll go home now and show my family all the things I can do with my new nose."

She thanked the old Baboon most politely and set off for home, frisking and whisking her new stretched nose, and thinking in a wondering sort of way about her new, stretched mind.

She walked straight and directly north across the dry and dusty Lowveld, scattered with baobab trees. Of course, the sun was hot and there was no shade and, thinking proudly of what she was doing, she schlooped up some mud from a water hole and sprayed it across her back and her neck so she wouldn't get sunburnt again. (And did you know, to this day elephants use mud as a sort of sunscreen?)

When she wanted fruit to eat, she pulled fruit down from a tree, and when she wanted grass, she plucked it from the ground as she walked. And when flies annoyed her, she broke a branch off a tree and used it as a fly-whisk. And when she felt lonely, she sang to herself through her trunk, and the noise was louder than several brass bands.

At last she reached her home just as the dark was settling in for the night. Her family were on their knees under a large marula tree, having a late afternoon grassy snack. The Elephant's Child coiled up her trunk and said, "Good evening, dear family."

They were overjoyed to see her and asked, "Have you satisfied your 'satiable curtiosity?"

"No," replied the Elephant's Child. "I most definitely have not. But let me show you what my 'satiable curtiosity has given me."

And, uncoiling her trunk, she reached down, pulled

up a clump of grass, dusted it against her front legs, and shoved it into her mouth. Then she reached up, plucked a few marula berries from the branches above her and ate them.

"Mmmm," she said. "Just ripe, but still retaining a little crunch. You ought to try them."

Then, seeing a horsefly on her uncle's shoulder, she said, "'Scuse me," most politely, stretched out her trunk and squashed the fly.

"There!" she said. "And if I need to call you, I now have a built-in trumpet."

And, curving her trunk up in the air, she sang down it hard, with a trumpeting noise that was louder than more than several brass bands.

"I want one!" demanded one of the Elephant's Child's little brothers.

"Ooh!" exclaimed one of her elephant aunts. "If we all had one, we could always talk to each other even if we're far apart. Imagine that!"

"How did you get it?" they all asked at once.

So the Elephant's Child told them her story. And they were all so excited that they made her lead them immediately and without hesitation to the banks of the great, grey-green, greasy Limpopo River, all set about with fever trees, to get new noses from the Crocodile.

And as they were coming back, the rains broke, and they spent the whole trip sploshing mud about with their trunks and eating delectable things they hadn't been able to eat before. And when the young elephants were tired of running around, they held onto their mother's tails with their new long noses, and felt safe and happy just plodding along, all in line with each other.

From that time on, all elephants have known that life is about more than just following each other around and eating grass. They talk and listen to each other constantly, with murmurs, and rumbles, and squeals, and trumpets. Each of them plays a part in helping the herd. They're curious and thoughtful. They support each other when times are tough.

So today, elephants are wise, and strong, and kind, and caring, true leaders in the African bush.

And all because the Elephant's Child showed them that if you want something better, you have to ask lots of curious questions, and as the wise old Chacma Baboon said, you have to stretch your mind so you can stretch your whole world.

Main Messages From the Fable:

The Five Principles of an Engaged Culture

In an Engaged Culture, people:

1. Share a clear, meaningful purpose

2. Work mainly in their areas of strength

3. Feel heard, respected, and recognised

4. Support each other when times are tough

5. Are encouraged to be curious, and to learn and grow

HOW THE LEOPARD GOT ITS SPOTS

Leading For a Culture That Embraces Change

(Loosely based on one of Rudyard Kipling's "Just So" Stories)

HOW THE LEOPARD GOT ITS SPOTS

In the long, long ago, soon after Africa had drifted away from the rest of Gondwana to be Africa all on its own, the leopard lived on the grey-gold savannah in the centre of that mystical and extended land. And the kudu, and the wildebeest, and the giraffe, and the zebra all lived there too.

But the leopard didn't climb trees, and he didn't creep through the forest undergrowth, and he didn't hunt in the darkness, as he does in these frenetical times. Now this may seem strange, because you might think he would do all those leopard-ish things when you consider his spottly, mottly coat that can blend and bend and disappear in the shadows.

But in those exotic times, Leopard's coat wasn't spottly and mottly at all. In fact, it had no spots whatsoever. It was a uniformly uniform grey-gold.

Now, all the others—Kudu, and Wildebeest, and Giraffe, and Zebra—also had uniform coats in sandy-ish, yellow-ish, brown-ish colours. But Leopard's coat was the smoothest and sleekest and the most uniform, without a patch, or a blotch, or a blemish. And he was very proud of it.

In fact, Leopard was a considerably conceited creature indeed. He liked to sit up on an antheap in the early morning sun, surveying the grasslands, and thinking vain thoughts about his sleek body and his even sleeker grey-gold coat.

"Look at my coat," he'd boast when Hyena stalked by, hoping for a meal to steal. "It's all smooth and sleek and not a spot in sight. Not all blotchy and rough and ragged like yours."

What Leopard liked most about his coat was that the grey-gold matched the grass of the sandy-coloured savannah perfectly to a hair. Now this was bad for Kudu, and Wildebeest, and Giraffe, and Zebra, because Leopard would lie behind a clump of that grey-gold grass and jump out and surprise them out of their sandy-coloured skins.

And of course, Kudu, and Wildebeest, and Giraffe, and Zebra were very fond of their skins, and they didn't much like being surprised out of them. It was very irksome.

So one fine day they all got together to decide what to do about it. And they came up with the cunningest of cunning plans. They all went together to see the great Mystical Barking Baboon, who lived alone on the top rocks of the highest hill on that vast and sweeping savannah.

They went together because, as they told each other, it was said that the great Mystical Barking Baboon knew everything, and if there were more of them, they could learn more. And, truth be told, they were a little afraid of him because he was wily, and wise, and mystically mystical and he could do magic.

"Oh, great Mystical Barking Baboon," said Kudu, and

HOW THE LEOPARD GOT ITS SPOTS

Wildebeest, and Giraffe, and Zebra, "we need your help. That smooth and sleek Leopard keeps surprising us out of our sandy-coloured skins, and we're sick of it. We want to be able to hide from him, or to see him better, or to go to where he isn't, but we don't know how to do that."

The wise old Mystical Barking Baboon looked at the four of them thoughtfully. "Have you thought and talked," he said, "about what things will be like, if you can hide from Leopard, or you can see Leopard better, or if you go to where Leopard isn't?"

"Yes!" they all said. "We most definitely have."

"And is that what you all want?" asked Baboon. "Have you all agreed on this?"

"Yes!" they all said. "We most definitely have."

"Then I can help you," said Baboon. "But if you can't all see for yourselves what things could be like, then making things change won't work. In fact," he said, "it might make things worse because you won't work together to make them change. You must all be sure you can see that things will be better."

"We do! We do!" they all exclaimed.

"Then come closer," said Baboon. "This is what we are going to do."

The next day when Leopard was sitting proudly on his antheap surveying the savannah, he saw that Kudu, and Wildebeest, and Giraffe, and Zebra weren't there, and that, he thought, was exceedingly surprising.

Well, Kudu, and Wildebeest, and Giraffe, and Zebra

weren't there the next day either, or the day after that, or the day after the day after that. And by then Leopard was as puzzled as a confused puzzle, and even more hungry than he was puzzled. He had hunted high, and he had hunted low, but those scarce and scrumptious animals were nowhere to be found.

After two weeks of eating beetles, and bugs, and worms, Leopard was fed up, and frustrated, and very hungry. So he also went to see the great Mystical Barking Baboon on the top rocks of the highest hill on that vast and sweeping savannah.

Now, Leopard was so conceited he had no room left inside his head for being afraid, and he bounded up to the top of the highest hill without hesitation.

"Great Mystical Barking Baboon," he began, looking up at Baboon sitting in his hairy, grey-brown skin, high on the highest rock. "Kudu, and Wildebeest, and Giraffe, and Zebra have all disappeared, and I'm as puzzled as a confused puzzle because I don't know where they've gone. Do you know where they are?"

The Mystical Barking Baboon smiled a knowing smile because he was wily and wise and mystically mystical. "Kudu, and Wildebeest, and Giraffe, and Zebra have gone into other spots," he said. "And my advice to you is to also go into other spots as soon as you possibly can."

"That's all very well," said Leopard. "But I need to know where they've gone."

"They've gone to where it's not uniformly uniform, to where there's no savannah, no grey-gold grass, because it was high time for a change. And my advice to you, oh uniformly one-coloured Leopard, is also to change as soon as you possibly can."

"I don't want to change," replied Leopard. "I just want to find Kudu, and Wildebeest, and Giraffe, and Zebra."

Baboon shrugged a knowing shrug. "Then you'll just have to go into other spots as you are. But there it's darker and deeper, and things are speckled and spottled, and splashed and slashed with shadows. And my advice to you would be to change before you go."

"I don't want to change," repeated Leopard. "I just want to find Kudu, and Wildebeest, and Giraffe, and Zebra. Will you take me to these other spots?"

"But I don't need to go to other spots," replied Baboon. "I'm already in them. And anyway, if I take you, once we get there, you might jump out at me and surprise me out of my hairy, grey-brown skin."

"If you will take me, I promise I won't jump out at you, or surprise you out of your skin in any way whatsoever," said Leopard.

The wise old Mystical Barking Baboon looked at Leopard for a few moments, thinking deep thoughts. Then he nodded three times in a meaningful sort of way.

"I will take you to find Kudu, and Wildebeest, and Giraffe, and Zebra. But do not forget your promise about no surprises, oh sleek and smooth Leopard," he warned.

So Leopard and Baboon walked north together for two days, to the very edge of the extended savannah, and there they saw a great, high, tall forest, full of trees, all speckled and spottled, and splashed and slashed with shadows, and not uniformly uniform at all.

Leopard was so hungry by then that he ran straight into those shadows and began searching. But after a few frantic hours, he came back out to where the Mystical Barking Baboon was patiently waiting.

"That's curious," said Leopard to Baboon. "I suppose it's because we have just come in out of the sunshine, but I can smell Zebra, and I can hear Zebra, but I can't see Zebra. And I can smell Kudu and I can hear Kudu, but I can't see Kudu. It's the same with all of them. It's excessively surprising—they seem to have no form."

"They seem to have no form because they have come into new spots," said Baboon. "So their form is blendable, and pliable, and infinitely flexible. They have become essentially adaptable. My advice to you, oh uniformly uniform Leopard, is to become essentially adaptable yourself as soon as possible."

But, Baboon thought to himself, *this conceited Leopard still won't want to change, and he won't want to become essentially adaptable because he thinks everything else should change so he can stay the way he is. And, anyway, he doesn't know how to change. So first he'll have to be shown that he won't be able to find Kudu, and Wildebeest, and Giraffe, and Zebra until he changes himself. And to do that, he'll have to learn that he* can *change himself.*

"I don't want to become adaptable," replied Leopard. "I just want to find Kudu, and Wildebeest, and Giraffe, and Zebra."

And wise old Baboon just smiled a knowing smile.

Then Leopard went back into the great high, tall forest and hunted all day. And though he could smell them and hear them, he never saw one of them.

"This is a scandal," he said to Baboon when he came out for afternoon tea. "I don't know whether it's really Kudu, and Wildebeest, and Giraffe, and Zebra in there because they have no form. I know what they sound like, and I can hear them. And I know what they smell like, and I can smell them. And I know what they look like, but I can't see them. I'll wait till after dark when they can't see me either."

So he waited till dark, and then he went back into the great, tall, high forest. After a short while, he heard something breathing in a softly snorting sort of way in the starlight that fell all stripy through the branches. And he jumped at the noise, and it smelt like Zebra, and it felt like Zebra, and when he knocked it down it kicked like Zebra, but he couldn't see it.

"Be quiet, you creature without any form," said Leopard. "I'm going to sit on your head till morning, because there is something about you I don't understand."

And he sat down hard on the creature without form and waited for morning.

When the morning sunlight was flickering all stripy and shimmery through the trees, Leopard looked at what he was sitting on. And he scratched his head in that more puzzled than a confused puzzle sort of way.

"You smell like Zebra, and you sound like Zebra, and you kick like Zebra. But you ought to be a creamy whitish-fawn all over, and you ought to be Zebra; but you're covered all over with blackish-greyish stripes. What in the world have you been doing to yourself, Zebra? Don't you know that on the grey-gold savannah I'll see you from a mile off?"

"Yes," replied Zebra. "But this isn't the grey-gold savannah. Can't you see?"

Leopard scratched his uniformly uniform head. "Oh, yes," he said. "That's true. I couldn't see it yesterday, but I can now. How did you do it?"

"Let me up," said Zebra, "and I'll call the others and we'll show you."

So the puzzled Leopard let Zebra get up, and Zebra called Kudu, and Wildebeest, and Giraffe, and they all came out into the clearing where Leopard could see them.

And Leopard stared in exceeding amazement. None of them had uniformly uniform skins anymore! Kudu was white-stripy down his sides, Wildebeest was black-stripy down *his* sides, and Giraffe was all covered in big chestnut blotches.

"Now watch," said Zebra. "This is how you do it. One… two… three! And where's your breakfast?"

Leopard stared and stared, but all he could see were the stripy, blotchy shadows of the forest, but never a sign of Zebra, or Kudu, or Wildebeest, or Giraffe. They had just walked off and hidden themselves in the trees.

Well, that's a lesson worth learning, thought Leopard. *I show up in this dark place like an elephant at a meeting of mice. I need to find out how to be temporaneously blendable.*

So he went out of the high, tall forest to where Baboon was sitting, smiling another knowing smile.

"So, oh smooth and sleek Leopard," said Baboon, "Have you at last become curious?"

"Yes, I'm more curious than a three-headed owl," replied

HOW THE LEOPARD GOT ITS SPOTS

Leopard. "And I've learned that I need to become blendable, and pliable, and essentially adaptable. I need to change into other spots. But how do I do that?"

"Isn't it wonderful what curiosity can do!" said Baboon. "But to become consistently blendable, and pliable, and essentially adaptable, you must also become infinitely learnable. That is undeniably critical."

The Leopard scratched his head, looking confusingly puzzled.

"Follow me," said Baboon. And turning on his tail, he set off in the opposite direction from the high, tall forest.

After some time, Baboon and Leopard reached the river, and Baboon made Leopard lie down on the grassy bank.

"Do you want stripes or spots?" Baboon asked, rubbing his hands in the murksome, sticky mud.

"Well," said Leopard, "you said I should go into spots. And I wouldn't want stripes. I wouldn't want to look like Zebra, or Kudu, or Wildebeest for anything! So spots it is. But I don't want them to be vulgar-large and blotchy like Giraffe. I wouldn't want to look like Giraffe for anything!"

"I'll make them small with the tips of my fingers," said Baboon.

And he put his five muddy fingers close together and pressed them all over Leopard, and wherever the five fingers touched, they left five little black marks, all close together. Sometimes his fingers slipped and the marks got a bit blurred, but there they were.

"Now you are a work of art!" said the Mystical Barking

Baboon. "Now you can be blendably blendable and essentially adaptable. But remember, oh conceited Leopard, you still have to be learnably learnable."

"Yes, yes…" said Leopard in a hungrily impatient, not really listening sort of way. "But let me try my new blendability."

And he climbed up the river bank to where the trees crowded out the sun and he simply disappeared. He truly did!

Baboon nodded, and he came up the bank to look more closely. And as he did that, that devious Leopard jumped out at him! But old Baboon was wily, and wise, and mystically mystical, and he leapt up into a tree as nimbly as a young baboon playing at a picnic.

"You promised you wouldn't do that, oh irksome Leopard," said Baboon from up on his branch. Then he fiddled his fingers and twirled his tail in a mystically magical sort of way.

And when he had finished twiddling and twirling, he said, "You'll have to go back into the deep, dark forest, you deceitful Leopard, and see if your blendability can find you breakfast there." Then he chuckled a knowing chuckle.

Well, Leopard went back and hunted in that forest for hours and hours. But he couldn't hear, or smell, or see Kudu, or Wildebeest, or Giraffe, or Zebra, not anywhere, or in any sense.

The great Mystical Barking Baboon sat on the outside of the forest and laughed. "Kudu, and Wildebeest, and Giraffe and Zebra aren't here, you uniformly ungrateful and unlearnable Leopard. Perhaps they've gone back to the grey-gold savannah. You'd better go there and find them before you starve!"

"But I'm all spotty," moaned Leopard. "I'll show up on my antheap on the grey-gold savannah like a giraffe in a meeting of meerkats. I'll have to go and wash these spots off in the river."

And he didn't like that idea at all, because, like most cats, Leopard didn't like getting wet.

Well, Leopard sat on the river bank and washed and washed, but the spots wouldn't come off. So he went right into the swirly water and he swam and he swam until he was so good at swimming he could catch fish. But those spots stayed as spottly as ever.

"You've put magic in these spots," he moaned to the Mystical Barking Baboon at last. "You've taken away my uniformly uniform grey-gold, smooth and sleek coat forever."

"Well then," replied Baboon, "my advice to you would be to carry on being blendable, and adaptable, and changeably changeable. And, as I said before, to do that you must learn to be infinitely learnable."

Then, chuckling another knowing chuckle, the Baboon set off back to the top rocks of the highest hill on the vast and sweeping savannah.

Leopard sat next to the river for the longest time, staring sadly at his spottly reflection. And as the wind rippled and ruffled the water, slowly he started to see something different in that reflection, something constantly changing, something pliable, and blendable, and essentially adaptable. Something that spread to be suddenly sensational!

Then at last he got up feeling positively positive and considerably not conceited, for he knew that wily and wise Baboon had taught him a learnable lesson.

So he set off back to the grey-gold savannah. And like his reflection in the rippling water, Leopard went on learnably learning, and changing and adapting.

He learned to climb trees where he could disappear in the shadowy branches. He learned to hunt in the stealth of the night, when the other animals couldn't see him in the dapply, patchy moonlight. He learned he could drag his meals up into a tree where that pesky hyena couldn't steal them.

And he found he loved being blendable, and adaptable, and changeably changeable. And he loved his new spots because he knew they'd given him something better.

The great Mystical Barking Baboon had been watching Leopard from the top rocks of the highest hill, and he saw him learn and change and grow in character. And he nodded a knowing nod.

This Leopard has learned the most important lesson of all, thought Baboon. *He's learned that he can be the one to make things changeably changeable. He's learned to be patently proactive. And so he's been rewardingly rewarded; everything's better for him than it was before, because now he can change on his own whenever he needs to.*

And over the years, Leopard taught his children what he had learned because now he knew the importance of being adaptably adaptable and learnably learnable. And he knew that sharing those learnings was imperatively important.

And to this day, all leopards love to swim and to catch fish, and they're blendable, and adaptable, and changeably changeable. And they know that's the best way to be.

But still today, in these adjustable times, the baboon doesn't quite trust the leopard. He had learned too!

Main Messages From the Fable:

The 5 Adaptation Habits for Leading Ongoing Change

1. Share a compelling vision

2. Involve and empower people

3. Encourage curiosity and continual learning

4. Recognise and reward proactivity

5. Share learnings from successes and failures

HOW THE MONKEY WAS HEARD

Communication is Key

HOW THE MONKEY WAS HEARD

IN THE LONG, LONG AGO, before the what of now, the southern parts of Africa were filled with great multitudes of animals. All manner of creatures lived in the grass and in the rocky outcrops and in the rivers and in the trees.

Those were chattering times and the savannah plains and woodlands were filled with snorts and grunts, and coughs and squawks, and chirps and squeals, and roars and rumbles. But one creature, a young vervet monkey called Shoko, was the biggest chatterer of all. He chattered all day, from dawn until dusk.

He chattered about how he was going to spend the day. He chattered about whether it would rain. He chattered about which were the tastiest wild fruits. But mostly he chattered about himself and how clever he was.

Now we must remember, Shoko *was* very clever. He knew lots of things, more than just about any other creature in those exotic times. And he was always learning new things to know. He learned how to knock down fruit from a tree with a stick, and he learned how to fish for termites with a stalk of grass, and he learned how to raid a beehive for honey without getting stung.

And he never stopped telling the other animals how much he knew and all the things he could do. And he annoyed everyone!

"There he goes again," Impala would say, "chattering on and on. 'Me… me… me!'"

"Yes," Tortoise would reply. "I know. It's alright for you. You can get away in a flash. Me… It takes me hours to get far enough away that I can't hear him. So now I just go into my shell and try to shut it out. I don't want to hear it anymore."

The young vervet monkey's family tried to talk to him.

"You mustn't talk about yourself so much, my dear," said his Great Aunt Inkawu. "It's not polite."

"That's right," said his Uncle Tumbili. "No-one likes a boastful monkey."

"But I've got so much I know," protested Shoko. "I want to show everyone all the things I've learned and all the things I can do."

"Well, that's very nice, dear," said his mother. "But maybe just tone it down a little. No-one listens to you any more, you know. Maybe talk about something else."

But Shoko didn't want to talk about something else. He wanted to talk about himself and all the things he knew. He was sure the others should all be learning from him.

It's important, he told himself. *After all, I'm much cleverer than anyone else. I've got so much I can show them, but they don't listen to me. And they should. I'm trying to help them. They could make things so much better for themselves if they tried to learn from me.*

He felt that if he kept telling them things often enough, maybe one day something would stick, and they'd try it. Then they'd see that he was right, and they'd also be able to knock down fruit from a tree with a stick, and to fish for termites with a stalk of grass, and to raid a beehive for honey without getting stung.

Late one day towards the end of a long, hot summer, just as dark was thinking about settling over the savannah, the monkey tribe was sitting together under a marula tree gossiping lazily as they browsed on fallen berries in the late afternoon heat. It was nearly time to climb up to bed, away from danger in the high branches.

Shoko was chattering away as usual, as he had been all day. Tortoise had gone into his shell in frustration and was trying to think of delicious green grass. Impala had flicked her white bob of a tail and bounced away to find a quieter spot. Porcupine, who had just woken up, scuttled back into his burrow and tried to go back to sleep. And the other monkeys just rolled their eyes, went on eating marula berries, and tried to ignore him.

"I can catch termites with a piece of grass," Shoko was saying. "I think I'm the only one who can do that. It's really easy if you practice."

"This is nearly the last of the berries," Great Aunt Inkawu said, totally ignoring Shoko. "The season seems to be finishing a little early this year."

"That's right," replied Uncle Tumbili. "It's been a very warm summer. I wonder what sort…"

"You just stick a long grass stalk into a hole in the termite mound," Shoko went on, "and a whole lot of termites grab onto the grass. Then you pull it out carefully and you can lick those termites off the grass all at the same time."

"… of winter it's going to be?" continued Uncle Tumbili. "Usually very cold after a warm summer."

"We may need to move a little north," suggested Great Aunt Inkawu, "to where…"

"It's so good!" Shoko looked around the group hopefully. "Does anyone want me to show them?"

"… it's a bit warmer and there's more to eat," his great aunt went on. "And we should go soon if it's going to be an early winter."

"Or I could you show you how to get honey without being stung?" Shoko offered.

For heaven's sake! thought Great Aunt Inkawu. *He needs to stop talking and listen for a change. Prattling on about termites and honey when we need to think about whether to move north for the winter. He thinks everything is all about him and how clever he is. He doesn't even try to understand what anyone else thinks or wants. It's intolerable!*

"Come over here where we can hear ourselves think!" she said to Uncle Tumbili, moving to the far side of the marula tree.

No-one noticed Ingwe the Leopard slipping silently through the long grass towards them.

A short while later, the monkey family were still browsing lazily, trying to ignore Shoko as they chatted among themselves.

Ingwe's mottled coat blended into the lengthening shadows.

"That young monkey looks delicious," she thought, her stomach rumbling in anticipation. "He'll be an easy catch, sitting their prattling away about himself."

She flexed her claws and inched slowly forward, crouched low and almost invisible in the long grass.

"I can knock down berries with a stick," said Shoko. "Does anyone want to see?"

But the other monkeys just went on munching berries.

Ingwe had stopped. She crouched perfectly still for a moment, her yellow-green eyes fixed on the young monkey. Then, in a dappled blur, she pounced!

Shoko had picked up a stick to show the others how he could knock the berries off a branch above him, but they were just out of reach. As he leaped up onto a lower branch to get closer, the leopard's claws raked across his back. He squealed in fear and pain. The other monkeys fled shrieking up into the high branches.

Shoko just managed to pull himself out of reach and jumped higher, too. The Leopard, knowing she had missed her meal, stalked away, rippling her coat in frustration.

Shoko sat shivering at the top of the marula tree. He hardly noticed the pain of the deep gashes down his side and across his back, but he hardly slept that night. His mind was in a whirl.

All the next day, and the day after that, Shoko sat up in the tree. He didn't eat, and he didn't say a word. Not one. He just sat there and stared ahead of him.

His family was dreadfully worried. His mother sat with him for hours licking his wounds to keep them clean while they healed, and gently grooming his coat. And she tried in vain to get him to eat something.

"Come along dear, here's a lovely, ripe fig. You love figs."

But it didn't work. Shoko still wouldn't eat and he wouldn't talk.

"He must have post-traumatic stress disorder," said Uncle Tumbili. "It's a bad thing that. He may never fully recover, you know."

Shoko hardly noticed his family's concern. Once he'd got over the initial shock, the close call with the leopard had really made him think. He'd spent the last two days thinking. He was still thinking. And he was a very clever monkey, remember.

Life was always risky in the African savannah, especially for a smallish, tasty creature like a vervet monkey. Monkeys were on the menu of lots of predators—leopards and hyenas on the ground, eagles from the air, snakes in the trees. They had to be alert and his incessant chatter about himself had been distracting them.

No matter how he tried to justify it, he realised that his boastful chattering had nearly made him the leopard's dinner. Worse still, it could have made one of his family the leopard's dinner!

I've been a very foolish monkey, he thought miserably. *All I wanted to do was share what I've learned and be helpful. But I've been making it all about me. And I haven't known when to stop or when to listen. If I want to help the others, it should be all about them. I should be listening to what they want first, then using what I know to be helpful in the way they need.*

Late in the afternoon on the third day after the Leopard's attack, the vervet monkey family were once again under their favourite marula tree, chatting lazily as they had their late afternoon snack. Shoko was still sitting high on his branch, thinking.

As he sat there, he noticed a movement in the long grass below him. Among the gently swaying shadows, he saw a mottled coat creeping slowly towards the tree. He saw a spotted tail twitch ever so slightly in the long grass. She was back!

"Leopard!" squealed Shoko. It was the first word he'd spoken in three days, and this time everyone listened.

The monkey family scampered up into the tree and Ingwe the Leopard, beaten again, glared balefully up at the young monkey before turning and stalking away.

The other monkeys clambered around Shoko.

"Thank goodness you were up there," said Great Aunt Inkawu.

"You're a real hero, son," said Uncle Tumbili, patting Shoko on the back.

"Oh, I was just in the right place at the right time," said Shoko, a little embarrassed. "And from now on, that's what I'm going to try to be—no more chattering about how clever I am. Just trying to be at the right place, at the right time, listening lots so I can see and understand more, and thinking before I speak so I can say the right things."

"Like '*Leopard*!'" chuckled Uncle Tumbili.

Shoko's mother gave him a big hug. "I'm just glad to have you back," she said.

"But a little less chatter and a lot more listening won't go amiss," said Great Aunt Inkawu, constructively honest as always.

"Yes," Shoko smiled ruefully. "And I think I know when to stop now. All it needed was that one word: 'Leopard!' That was enough."

"Well, you've learned a useful lesson then," said Great Aunt Inkawu. "And maybe that lesson goes for all of us."

"You're right," said Uncle Tumbili. "And, you know, I think I would like to learn a lesson too. It would be good to know how to fish for termites."

"Oh, it's not that hard," exclaimed Shoko. "You just take a piece of grass and…" He stopped suddenly. "Sorry," he said sheepishly. "Tell me when you'd like to try, Uncle Tumbili, and I'll show you how to do it if you would like me to."

"Mmmm…," pondered Great Aunt Inkawu. "Maybe we could all have a lesson together. That would be good for all of us. A real win-win."

And the next day, that's exactly what they did.

From that day on, all vervet monkeys have learned to knock down fruit from a tree with a stick, and to fish for termites with a stalk of grass, and to raid a beehive for honey without getting stung. And while they still chatter among themselves, they don't try to dominate the conversation, and they don't make it all about themselves.

Now, they often sit high in the trees and warn the other animals if an eagle is flying overhead, or a leopard is stalking close by, or a snake is winding its way through the branches.

They're the alarm call in the African bush. So now, when vervet monkeys talk, everyone listens because they know it'll be worth hearing!

Main Messages From the Fable:

> ## The Five Principles of Effective Communication
>
> 1. First, listen to understand
>
> 2. Make it about them, not you
>
> 3. Know when to stop
>
> 4. Be open and constructively honest
>
> 5. Always seek a win-win

CONCLUSION

LEADERSHIP VERSUS MANAGEMENT

Some of the fables in this book point to the difference between management and leadership. It's an important distinction. One of the central keys to good leadership is this:

Lead people, manage processes.

While effective processes are important in supporting people to do their work, life can be made much easier for any executive, manager, supervisor, or team leader if they have the willing cooperation of the people implementing those processes.

And if the leadership style and corporate culture promote self-leadership and at least a degree of empowerment in employees, the people whose role it is to implement those processes are likely to look for ways to improve them.

Given the constant and rapid change we now live with in every industry, regularly reviewing and improving or changing processes, or perhaps the entire work function, is essential for effectiveness and often for survival.

When the people implementing the processes are the ones seeking to improve them, it reduces change resistance and ensures buy-in, because it's human nature to more readily accept something we ourselves have developed or contributed to.

Importantly, allowing people the opportunity to have greater control over the design of their role, the use of their natural strengths, and the processes that support them, are critical keys to improving employee engagement, corporate culture, and mental wellness in the workplace. We all have a need to be trusted, respected, valued, and recognised.

Our organisations urgently need to shift from a process management and control perspective to a Self-Led Leadership perspective. For those that don't, the future is likely to hold the unsustainable time, effort, and monetary costs of low staff retention, difficulty with talent acquisition, poor corporate culture, low employee engagement, and low productivity. The ultimate result will be a poor corporate image and declining profitability.

Showing trust, respect, value, and recognition to others is the only way to continue to learn, grow, and improve as individuals, as teams, as organisations, as communities, as a species. It requires the spirt of "Ubuntu", the Nguni Bantu term, which roughly translates as: "I am me because we are we." And that spirit must come from the top. The principles of Self-Led Leadership apply to the board director as much as to the sales assistant, but if it's not espoused at senior levels, it's unlikely to gain much traction on the shop floor.

And we need to apply Ubuntu thinking not just to our organisations and other people, but also to the many and varied other species that jointly determine the future of life on our planet. That, in part, is why I love using animal fables to convey essentially human messages.

We're just starting to understand the crucial links between the myriad species on Earth, and the interdependence of those species for their survival, including our own. But that's a topic perhaps for another book.

I hope the fables in this book have inspired you, sparked your curiosity, and fuelled your determination to learn and grow alongside others as a leader and a human being. And, importantly, I hope it has entertained you.

Walk gently in this world, knowing you are strong enough to fulfil your own dreams and to support the worthwhile dreams of others.

ABOUT JOHN ANDREW CARROLL

John Carroll grew up surrounded by wildlife and war in Zimbabwe in southern Africa. With degrees in business and psychology, he is an experienced CEO and managing director in both commercial and non-profit organisations, a university lecturer, an award-winning leadership trainer, an international professional speaker, and the author of three books on leadership and self-leadership and currently working on his first novel, also themed on African animals.

He has lived and worked on three continents, founded his own successful advertising agency from which not one staff member resigned in 7 years, is on the board of directors of various organisations, and recently led a large human services company through the successful merging of 12 separate organisations in four years to achieve global top-tier staff satisfaction and engagement ratings just one year after the main merger.

Fuelled by his passion for people, wildlife and environmental issues, John is a founding member of TheBEATS.org, a growing non-profit organisation that focuses on biodiversity and endangered and threatened species to help connect people in Australia more closely with nature.

Connect with John

www.johncarroll.com.au
john@johncarroll.com.au
www.linkedin.com/in/johncarrolltalk
www.facebook.com/johncarrollaus

ACKNOWLEDGEMENTS

So many people have helped create this book.

I can't name everyone who has helped in some way to shape my understanding of leadership, because my lessons and experiences, good and bad, have come from a multitude of sources: my parents, teachers, employees, jobs, bosses, colleagues, mentors, students, clients, organisations, books, training… the list goes on. But I acknowledge and thank every one of you.

For the storylines and writing style of some of the fables (as noted in the relevant fable titles), I must acknowledge the works of Rudyard Kipling (1865–1936). Kipling, now somewhat controversial due to his interpretation of how the British empire was experienced, was, I believe, a great writer nonetheless—he was awarded the Nobel Prize in Literature in 1907. His books and short stories, especially those about animals, like The Jungle Book and the Just So Stories, and his poems, "Gunga Din," "If-," "Mandalay," and many others, certainly inspired me to write as a boy.

No book can reach its finished product stage without support and input from other people. Thanks to the team at Balboa Press for your as-ever professional work. To my family, Sue, Jamie, and Sarah, my friend, Tom Schumann, and my brother and sister-in-law, Simon and Jann Carroll, thanks for your encouragement, support, proofreading, beta reading, and invaluable ideas, comments, and suggestions.

And finally, to you, the reader, thank you for choosing this book. I hope you have enjoyed it, and perhaps learned something about and from the creatures that inhabit its pages. We're all in this world together, including them, so let's go out there and make it the best world we can for every one of us.

www.ingramcontent.com/pod-product-compliance
Lightning Source LLC
Chambersburg PA
CBHW020435220526
45464CB00002B/712